WITHDRAWN
HARVARD LIBRARY
WITHDRAWN

Lead, Radiant Spirit

Our Gospel Quest

John Navone

Lead, Radiant Spirit

Lead, Radiant Spirit
Our Gospel Quest

John Navone, S.J.

A Liturgical Press Book

THE LITURGICAL PRESS
Collegeville, Minnesota

www.litpress.org

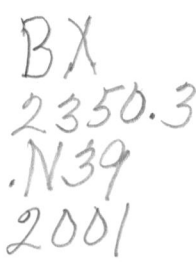

Cover design by Ann Blattner. *The Baptism of Christ* by Piero della Francesca.

Unless otherwise indicated, all scriptural quotations in the text are paraphrases or translations provided by the author.

© 2001 by The Order of St. Benedict, Inc., Collegeville, Minnesota. All rights reserved. No part of this work may be reproduced in any form or by any means, electronic or mechanical, including photocopying, recording, taping, or any retrieval system, without the written permission of The Liturgical Press, Collegeville, MN 56321. Printed in the United States of America.

1   2   3   4   5   6   7   8   9

Library of Congress Cataloging-in-Publication Data

Navone, John J.
    Lead, radiant spirit : our gospel quest / John Navone.
      p.   cm.
    Includes bibliographical references and index.
    ISBN 0-8146-2594-0 (alk. paper)
    1. Christian life—Catholic authors.   2. Spiritual life—Catholic Church.
    3. Christian life—Biblical teaching.   4. Spiritual life—Biblical teaching.
    5. Bible. N.T. Gospels—Theology.   6. Catholic Church—Doctrines.
    I. Title.

BX2350.3 .N39   2001
248.4'82—dc21

00-052041

Contents

Introduction   1

   Light and Darkness   1
   Biblical Tensional Symbolism   5
   The World of Desire and the World of Limits   11
   The Paradigm: Jesus, Religious Authorities, Disciples   18
   Excursus: Religious Consciousness and the
      Language of Interiority   19

Chapter 1
Mark: Transfigured or Disfigured?   23

   "God alone is good" (Mark 10:18)   23
   "You think not the things of God, but human things"
      (Mark 8:33)   24
   Traits of the Disciples   26
   Traits of the Religious Authorities   30
   Conflicting Desires   34
   Living in God's Love   35
   Baptism, Transfiguration, the Cross:
      Signs of Acceptance   38
   Baptism and Transfiguration   40
   The Cross: Locus of Divine Love   42
   Excursus: Conflict Stories in Mark   45

Chapter 2
Matthew: God's Righteousness or Self-Righteousness?   47

   God's Happiness   47
   Doing God's Will   49

The Greater Righteousness: Be Perfect! 52
Justice and Mercy 53
Righteousness as Gift 56
The Law of Love 58
Pulls and Counterpulls within the Community 59
The Call to Vigilance 62

Chapter 3
Luke: Banquet Joy or Resentment? 65

God's Peace, Joy, and Salvation for All 65
The Traits of Jesus 70
The Traits of the Disciples 72
The Traits of the Religious Authorities 74
God in Daily Life 78
Summons to Conversion 79
Becoming Merciful/Compassionate 81
Excursus: Lukan Themes 84
"Parable of the Prodigal Son Invites Us to Rejoice over Repentant Sinners" 85
The Ungracious Refuser of Happiness/Salvation 89

Chapter 4
John: God's Glory or Self-Glorification? 93

Opposed Ways of Self-Understanding 93
Love and Faith 93
Love of the Darkness (Loves Opposed to Faith): John 3:16-21 95
Love for Human Glory: John 12:43 96
Love for One's Own Life: John 12:25 97
Love of the World: 1 John 2:15-16 98
Love for the Glory of God (Loves Associated with Faith): John 12:43 99
Love for the Light: John 3:19 101

Love for Christ: John 8:42-47   102
Love of God: John 5:40-44 and 1 John 2:15   103
Cosmic Conflict   103
The Gift and Call of God to Glory
  (in the Glorified Christ)   106
Two Schemes of Gospel Thought   108
  1. Cosmic Conflict in Johannine Thought   108
  2. The Holy Spirit of Reciprocal Love   109

Chapter 5
The Universal Pilgrimage to the Mountain of God   111

  Conversion Paradigm   111
  The Universal Pilgrimage to the Mountain of God   112
  Five Aspects of the Universal Pilgrimage   113
    1. The Epiphany of God   113
    2. The Call of God   114
    3. The Journey of the Gentiles   115
    4. Worship at the World-Sanctuary   116
    5. The Messianic Banquet on the Mountain of God   117
  New Testament Fulfillment of Pilgrimage Prophecy   118
    1. Epiphany/Christophany/Theophany   119
    2. The Call of God in Christ   119
    3. Jesus Is the Way   120
    4. Jesus Is the Temple/Universal Sanctuary of God   120
    5. Jesus' Eschatological Messianic Banquet   121
  Excursus: Jesus the Way   122
  Excursus, Part II:
    From Paradise Lost to Paradise Regained:
    The Garden and the Wilderness Metaphors   124
  The Universal Pilgrimage to the Mountain of God as a
    Paradigm of the Universal Call to Conversion   127

Introduction

The tensional structure of human life as a field of pulls and counterpulls is a key to understanding the symbolic biblical narratives about life in the community of faith. *Lead, Radiant Spirit* examines the tensional structure of theocentric life in the community of faith both in terms of biblical literature about that life and of contemporary studies in related fields.

The title discloses some of the author's presuppositions about the tensional structure of theocentric life in the community of faith. "Lead" is a prayer. There is no theocentric life without prayer. Secondly, it is a prayer based on the conviction that an all-loving and all-merciful God hears our cries for a salvation that we cannot obtain for ourselves. The "Radiant Spirit" is the *Mysterium tremendum et fascinans:* the light, the joy, the beauty and the marvel of the Supreme Good of our lives and the Common Good of all life. It is the "Radiant Spirit" that inspires the psalmist:

> You will show me the path of life, the fullness of joy in your presence, at your right hand happiness for ever (6:11).
>
> The Lord is my light and my salvation; whom shall I fear? (27:1).

Light and Darkness

The light and darkness symbolism of the Bible reflects the tensional structure of human life. The contrast between light and darkness derived in the first place from the alternation of day and night, that is, from the natural rhythm of light and darkness in the ordinary sense. This temporal division, which is an element in the world order, is something given by God and contributes to the glorification of God the Creator. With the creation of light and the division between light and darkness God brought to an end the primordial condition of chaos (Gen 1:3-4) and right from the beginning the work of creation moves forward according to this alternating rhythm of day and night.

This order has been created with reference to our salvation (Ps 104:23); therefore, when it is violated or destroyed it is a sign of divine punishment for the sins of humankind. Darkness by daytime will proclaim the great day of judgment, the "day of Yahweh" (see Jer 4:23, 28; Amos 8:9; Joel 2:2, 31; 3:14). Since the daytime and light are experienced as the time of life, of activity and happiness, the morning or, in other texts, the rising sun, are greeted as bringing blessing from God on their arrival (Pss 3:5-6; 5:3; 46:5; 57:3; 90:14; 130:6–143:8; Isa 33:2; Zeph 3:5). Night is the time of lamentation and sighing (e.g., Pss 30:5; 77:2; 119:147). The Israelite, who loves life, can only represent the kingdom of the dead, the underworld, as the land of darkness and shadow (Pss 45:19; 88:11-12; Job 10:21-22; 38:17; Eccl 6:4-5).

The metaphorical and symbolic application of light and darkness to the tensional structure of life in the community of faith expresses various meanings in the biblical tradition. Living in the light signifies happiness; light and life belong together as do darkness and death, darkness and damnation (cf. Pss 56:13; 97:11; Job 22:28; 30:26). This ordinary symbolism is seen as religious because God is the source of light and life—"for with you is the fountain of life; in your light do we see light" (Ps 36:9), meaning that we receive from God happiness and salvation (cf. Ps 18:28; 118:27; Isa 9:1; Mic 7:8), an idea which squares with the concept of the "glory" of God as described eschatologically (Isa 60:1-3, 19-20; 62:1-2; 66:18-19; Zech 2:5, 8). To *walk in the light* refers to the direction in which one walks, *the right way,* for it is the "light" of the Lord which leads the pious Israelite (Ps 43:3; Job 29:3; Isa 2:51; Mic 7:8). In this way "light" becomes a metaphor for *the law of God* (Ps 119:105; Prov 6:23; Wis 18:4) and for *wisdom* (Eccl 2:13; Bar 4:1-2).

There is a wide variety in the metaphorical use of the terms light and darkness in the New Testament. There is a generally recognizable constant that where God is and where God reveals Godself in theophany or christophany there is light (see Luke 2:9; Matt 17:2, 5 and parallels; 28:3; Acts 1:10; 9:3; 10:30; 12:7). The great revelation of salvation, however, consists in this, that "the people who sat in darkness have seen a great light" (Matt 4:16; quoted from Isa 9:2). The light of God for those in the shadow of death is Jesus Christ himself, the Messiah, the "light for revelation to the Gentiles" (Luke 2:32), a title which had already been applied to the Servant of the Lord in the Songs of the Servant (Isa 42:6; 49:6). The light of God can also refer to "the gospel of the glory of Christ" or, finally, to God who through Christ and his good tidings of salvation has shone forth in our hearts like the light of the morning of creation (2 Cor 4:4-6; 2 Tim 1:10). God has called even pagans from the darkness into his marvelous light (1 Pet 2:9).

Light is a constant figure for the salvation which comes in as the eschatological reality with Christ and finds its completion in the future kingdom of God. "To be thrown into the outer darkness" means to be excluded from the banquet hall of God (which is full of light), that is, from his eschatological kingdom (Matt 8:12; 22:13; 25:30). In one case darkness is even represented as an evil power which is active and aggressive; in the text in which Jesus says on being arrested, "this is your hour, and the power of darkness" (Luke 33:53). Similarly in Ephesians 6:12 those angelic powers which have rebelled against God and which threaten the salvation of humankind are called "the world rulers of this present darkness."

One who answers the call of Christ becomes "a child of the light." Jesus contrasts the "sons of light" with the "sons of this age" (Luke 16:8). He calls his disciples "the light of the world" (Matt 5:14). Early Christian preaching gives great importance to the warning about living one's life in the light (see Rom 13:12; Eph 5:8; 1 Thess 5:4-6; 1 John 1:7; 2:9-10). Paul asks "What fellowship has light with darkness? What accord has Christ with Belial?" (2 Cor 6: 14-15). Paul explains how Satan can disguise himself as an angel of light (2 Cor 11:14). Paul affirms that God the Father has "qualified us to share in the inheritance of the saints in light . . . and delivered us from the dominion of darkness" (Col 1:12-13).

In John's writings the concept of light and the dualism between light and darkness come through most clearly. Here Christ refers to himself as "the light of the world" (John 8:12; 9:5). One who follows him in faith does not walk in darkness (that is, in this present earthly cosmos estranged from God) but will have "the light of life" (8:12); he will not stumble and fall (11:9-10) but will become a "child of the light" (12:36). Identical with Godself, the preexistent *logos* was the 'light of humankind' whom the darkness could not overcome (1:4-5) neither in the preexistent stage nor when the incarnate *logos* came into this darkened world for the salvation of humankind (12:46). The guilt of humankind consisted loving the darkness more than the light (3:19) on account of dualism of the world of light and the world of darkness (reality vs. unreality; meaningfulness vs. meaninglessness; happiness vs. desolation; life vs. death; love vs. unlove; truth vs. illusion; fulfillment vs. self-destruction) is the context for Christ's mission of offering to all the possibility of participating in the light and life of God. Christ's call to walk in the light is a call to love the brethren (John 2:9); without this love the affirmation that one is "in the light," that is, a friend of God, is a lie. God is light in whom there is no darkness (John 1:5); for God is love in whom there is no unlove. The unloving cannot claim to have communion with Love Itself.

Beginning with Christ and by means of Christ who is the "true light" (John 1:9), and also by means of Christians who have welcomed his light and life within themselves and communicate it through fraternal love, God's kingdom of light spreads outwards and God's radiant Spirit overcomes the darkness (John 2:8).

"Pillar of fire and of cloud" is a composite phrase for biblical symbolism that especially captures the meaning of *Lead, Radiant Spirit*.

This composite phrase appears in the story of the Exodus (Exod 14:24), and there are a number of occurrences of the separate phrases, "pillar of cloud" (Exod 13:21-22 and six times elsewhere in the Old Testament) and "pillar of fire" (Exod 13:21-22; Num 14:14; Neh 9:12, 19). The pillar meets Israel at the edge of the wilderness and continues thereafter with Israel in the desert. It is a theophany of cloud and glory, a symbol of the divine presence guiding and protecting the People of God in the wilderness. The cloud by day and the fire by night advance in front of the Israelites, and show them their way, giving them a continuous and perpetual guidance (Exod 13:21-22). The pillar of cloud moves from before to the rear of Israel, separating the Egyptians from the Israelites, thus protecting and saving the latter (Exod 14:19-20).

The cloud occasionally descends to stand at the door of the tent of meeting outside the camp. When this took place, there was converse between Yahweh and Moses. The pillar of cloud was a place of revelation, protection, and divine presence. It is the glory of the tabernacling presence of God among God's people. "Glory" and "God" occasionally become synonymous in the Old Testament (Exod 33:22; Lev 9:4, 6, 23; Ps 113:4; Zech 8:2).

Pillar of Fire and of Cloud is associated with the Old Testament symbolism of light. Created prior to and independent of the heavenly luminaries (Gen 1:3-5), light is the most general and most adequate manifestation of divine operation in a world which apart from it is darkness and chaos. The ancient Hebrews did not differentiate between natural and supernatural light. The phenomenon of dawn prior to sunrise was to them evidence that God pursued a special purpose in creating this world. The dawn indicates that darkness will not last and reign forever (e.g., Ps 130:6; Hos 6:3, 5). Light is therefore the essence of all the gifts through which God blesses God's creatures.

Biblical Tensional Symbolism

Biblical narratives symbolize human existence as a field of pulls and counterpulls. The Gospel of John uses the word, draw, drag *(helkein)*. Jesus, on the eve of his passion, can say, "And I shall draw all men to myself, when I am lifted up" (12:32). But the power of the crucified and risen Lord to draw humankind to himself is conditioned by the prior drawing by the Father: "No man can come to me unless he is drawn by the Father who sent me" (6:44). And that prior drawing entails a listening and a learning: "Everyone who has listened to the Father and learned from him, comes to me" (6:45). Nobody can recognize the movement of the divine presence in the Son, unless he is prepared for such recognition by the presence of the divine Father in himself.

Biblical narratives affirm the precariousness of human existence within the field of pulls and counterpulls. In Matthew's Gospel Jesus affirms: "For whoever would save his life will lose it; and whoever loses his life for my sake will find it. What then will it profit a man, if he gains the whole world but has to suffer the destruction of his life" (16:25f.). Or again one may read in Paul: "If you live according to the flesh, you are bound to die; but if by the spirit you put to death the deeds of the body, you will live" (Rom 8:15). A variant appears in John's Gospel: "The hour has come for the Son of Man to be glorified. In truth, in very truth I tell you, a grain of wheat remains a solitary grain unless it falls into the ground and dies; but if it dies, it bears a rich harvest. The man who loves himself is lost, but he who hates himself in this world will be kept safe for eternal life" (12:23ff.).

In brief, there is within the tensional structure of human interiority a pull or attraction that, if followed, leads to human fulfillment/happiness. There is also a counterpull or attraction that, if followed, leads to self-destruction/unhappiness.

The tensional structure of human interiority underlies human progress and decline. Progress proceeds from perfect and universal fidelity to the exigencies of self-transcendence: Be attentive, Be intelligent, Be reasonable, Be responsible.[1] Precisely because the invariant structure of that transcendence is dynamic, it yields the basic unit of a circle of progress.

Precepts may be violated. Decline results from the violation of the transcendental precepts. It compromises and distorts progress. Inattention, obtuseness, unreasonableness, and irresponsibility produce objectively absurd situations that do not yield to treatment. Corrupt minds have a flair for picking the mistaken solution and insisting that it alone is intelligent, reasonable, good. As self-transcendence promotes progress, so the refusal of self-transcendence turns progress into cumulative decline.[2]

---

[1] Bernard Lonergan, *Method in Theology,* 2nd ed. (New York: Herder & Herder, 1972) 53. The precepts entail attention to human affairs, a grasp of hitherto unnoticed or unrealized possibilities, and basing one's decisions on an unbiased evaluation of costs and benefits.

[2] Ibid., 53–55.

Human interiority is a distinct area of reality and the mode of human participation in all reality. It is the site of what may be characterized as a polar dynamism. Our subjectivity is present to itself in a conscious process delineated by poles of tension.[3] Such a process underlies our knowing, for prior to knowledge is the conscious attitude of questioning that relates us to what is not yet known: the knower and the to-be-known are polarities between which conscious movement is consciously experienced.

Our consciousness is luminous in so far as it gives rise to paired symbolic doublets that express the intentional experience of its own tensional structure. Splitting such pairs resolves the tension and makes accessible to static construction what is essentially dynamic. Reason intends far more than what is available through sense data. It cannot be equated with logic, nor with a faculty that somehow "belongs" to the human subject. A depth or ground or "Beyond" is present in the immediate movements of the human spirit. Our consciousness becomes luminous to itself as the site of seeking and being drawn, such that the seeking and being drawn, the questioning itself, is an experience of the Mystery that both grounds our existence and is not detachable from that existence. Pairs of symbols are indispensable for expressing our intentional experience of our tensional structure: imperfection/perfection, mortality/immortality, death/life, human/divine.

Bernard Lonergan, evaluating the thought of Eric Voegelin, insists how right he considers Voegelin to be in what he says about the kind of knowledge by which people live their lives.[4] It is the kind of knowledge that scientists and scholars, philosophers and theologians, presuppose when they perform their special tasks. It is the knowledge of which Newman wrote in his *Grammar of Assent,* Polanyi wrote in his *Personal Knowledge,* Gadamer in his *Truth*

---

[3] Eric Voegelin describes human existence as "existence-in-metaxy," a movement that occurs in the "in-between" delineated by the poles of tension in human consciousness. "Reason: The Classic Experience," *The Southern Review* 10 (April 1974); "Equivalences of Experience and Symbolization in History," in *Eternità e Storia* (Firenze: Vallechi, 1970).

[4] "Theology and Praxis," in the Catholic Theological Society of America, Proceedings of the Thirty-Second Annual Convention (1977) 6–10.

and Method. It is the kind of knowledge thematized by ascetical and mystical writers when they speak of the *discernment* of spirits and set forth rules for distinguishing between pull and counterpull, between being drawn by the Father to be drawn to the Son and, on the other hand, the myriad other attractions that distract the human spirit.

It is in this long history of spiritual writing that Lonergan finds the confirmation of Voegelin's "In-Between" and his "Beyond." For being drawn by the Father is neither merely human nor strictly divine but "In-Between." As movement is from the mover but in what is moved, so the drawing is from the Father but in the suppliant.[5] Again, because the drawing is from the Father, it bears the stamp of unworldliness; it is not just me but from the "Beyond." Finally, because there are not only pulls but also counterpulls, because the first can dignify the second, and the second can distort the first, there is need for discernment and, no less, difficulty in attaining it.

Voegelin's notion of reason takes its stand on our inner experience of the pulls and counterpulls within us, like Paul in Romans 7. The dialectical tension between the pull of grace and counterpull is the very stuff of discernment in the lives of Christians seeking to learn what God requires of them.

The truth, known in the dynamics of consciousness, that our existence is indeed existence in tension toward the Known Unknown achieves articulation in the temporal symbolism of narrative. Such symbolism is indispensable for expressing our relationship to the Mystery that is ultimately intended in every operation of our intentional consciousness, the restlessness that continues to raise questions of truth and of value even when questions about the world of space and time have been put to rest. If we continue to ask questions—if we continue to be human—our questioning will eventually reach the question of God: that which is intended in the dynamic of questioning is transcendent Being.[6]

---

[5] Ibid., 14.

[6] Bernard Lonergan, *Method in Theology*, 2nd. ed. (New York: Herder & Herder, 1972) 110.

Our religious narratives are born out of the spontaneous conviction that order prevails over chaos, that the absurd is not the final word, that reality is intelligible. Meaning is not experienced, lived, and felt outside some narrative framework.

The case for God's reality may be argued not simply in a primal, interpersonal, pre-theoretical way but also in a "post-theoretical" way on the basis of our awareness of our desire to know.[7] The basic condition necessary to call forth our questioning is that reality is intelligible. Our questioning spontaneously posits that there is intelligibility to be grasped in a universe that is fully intelligible and has an ultimate explanation. Otherwise we would not have sought it out. There would be no questioning without the anticipation or foreknowledge, however hazy, of some answer.

The literary language of the Bible is distinct from the technical language of theology.[8] The symbolic narratives, prayers, and poetry of the Bible are not attempts at achieving "scientific" knowledge.[9] They express the primordial religious knowledge that is the matrix for conceptual theological knowledge. The literary language of the Bible expresses the primordial religious knowing of the community of faith; the technical language of theology expresses the conceptual knowing of that same community. Both forms of knowing and their corresponding expressions of meaning have their own excellencies.[10] Primordial is foundational for all knowing; it clings to particulars and individuals, and plumbs their mysteries. It never moves far from the vibrancy, feeling and intimate involvement of immediate experience. Conceptual knowing is precise and articulate. It lends itself to definition and logic. It heads toward system, and permits scientific statements. The community of faith needs both kinds of knowing and their corresponding expressions

---

[7] John F. Haught, *Religion and Self-Acceptance* (New York/Paramus/Toronto: Paulist Press, 1976) 132.

[8] See David Tracy, *The Achievement of Bernard Lonergan* (New York: Herder & Herder, 1970) 217f.

[9] There is a range of meanings in the literary language of the Bible which technical scientific language can no more capture than can prose express the power of poetry.

[10] Terry Tekippe, *Scientific and Primordial Knowing* (Lanham/New York/London: University Press of America, Inc., 1996) 478.

of meaning to communicate its common store of common experiences, common understandings, common judgments, and common decisions.

The community of faith employs the literary language of the Bible for the transformation and maturation of its members. In the literary art of the Bible, content cannot be separated from form. If the biblical authors are calling for a change in the assumptions, interests, and concerns of their hearers and readers, the dimensions of this change must be clarified by careful study of the language of the call. The transformation sought is reflected in the language used. We encounter "tensive language" in the Bible: language which embodies a tension and expresses a conflict with ordinary ways of thinking and acting.[11] Study of the language helps us to locate the primary point of tension and explore the strategies used to encourage religious conversion both as event and lifelong process. Not only the explicit commands are a call and a challenge for theocentric self-transcendence (religious conversion), for statements and stories may also contain hidden imperatives and invitations to change.

The tensive language of the Bible presents God's purpose for humankind in conflict with the obstacles to God's purpose. Because God is Happiness Itself, the tensive language of the Bible appropriately symbolizes human existence as a field of pulls towards and counterpulls away from Happiness Itself.[12]

Jesus Christ, in John's Gospel, reveals and communicates the Spirit of Happiness Itself (15:11; 16:24), a gift no one else can give us, a treasure that no one can take from us (16:22). The gift of his Spirit is the peace of Happiness Itself: "Peace be with you . . . receive the Holy Spirit" (20:19, 22). The radiant Spirit of Happiness Itself is the reciprocal love of the Father and Son whose beauty/glory saves the world: "The glory that you have given me I have given them, so that they may be one, as we are one" (17:22-23).

---

[11] This phrase is used by Philip Wheelwright, *Metaphor and Poetry* (Bloomington, Ind.: Indiana University, 1962) 45–69.

[12] Aquinas refers to God as "Happiness Itself" in the *Summa Theologiae* I–II q. 3, a. 2. God's very being is God's being happy. Whatever God is, is God's happiness; this is not something extrinsic to God, but the very life or eternal activity of God.

There is a cosmic conflict in John's Gospel between Jesus and the "prince of this world" (12:31; 16:11). In the cosmic dialectic between good and evil, experienced in all human life, the Way, the Truth, and the Life of Happiness Itself (14:6; 15:11) meets with rejection (1:11) and hatred (15:18). To reject the incarnate Word and Spirit of Happiness Itself entails a form of self-destruction (8:21, 24). But to all who welcome that Word and Spirit was given the power to enjoy Happiness Itself (1:12).

Because God's love has been poured into our hearts through the Holy Spirit which has been given to us (Rom 5:5), we are able to see with the eye of love that is Christian faith and to enjoy with the look of love that is Christian contemplation the beauty of God's self-giving love displayed towards all humankind in the gift of Jesus Christ and which Christ himself displayed in his relations with his Father and with his fellow human beings. The Holy Spirit, dwelling within us as the foretaste and promise of what God has prepared for those who love God, shows us the Father's love in Christ and gives us the hope of unending joy.

The mystery of God's saving purpose for humankind (e.g., Mark 4:11; Rom 11:25; 16:25-27; Col 1:25-27; 4:3; Eph 1:9-10; 3:1-12; 6:19; 1 Tim 3:16) has been revealed through Christ and is being completed in the Spirit. The Christian community of faith confesses that Jesus Christ is God the Father's incarnate Son, upon whom the Spirit rests and at whose prayer the Father pours the Spirit upon us that our sins may be forgiven and we may be conformed to Christ and transformed according to God's image for our eternal happiness and God's own glory. The Christian community's joy in the Holy Spirit (e.g., Luke 10:21; Acts 13:52; Rom 14:17) is the promise and assurance of future joy (John 16:20, 22). It is evidence that the Lord is even now calling God's faithful servants into God's joy without end (Matt 5:12): eternal life with Happiness Itself.

The World of Desire and the World of Limits

The tensional structure of human life and its biblical symbolism can be grasped in terms of the two "worlds" in which the human being may be said to live: the "world of desire" and the "world of limits."[13] These worlds have contrasting and divergent characteristics. There is a world of imagination, of inquiry, and of desire in general, which is potentially unlimited, and which can continue to enlarge as life proceeds. There is also a world of inescapable limits, which become more constricted as time passes. Thus, a tension prevails between these two worlds, a tension arising already in early childhood, which, insofar as the person confronts it, becomes more explicit as life goes by. Much depends on whether this tension is resolved, and on how it is resolved.

Even though it may not be experienced in a constantly acute way, a tension between the world of desire and the world of limits must be seen as inevitable unless one assumes that one can attain everything that one might desire, which is absurd, because it implies omnipotence. Life involves a continuous frustration of wishes tending to omnipotence. One who has ever lamented the inadequacy of one's resources in pursuing even perfectly valid goals has experienced what seems to be the irreducible minimum of such frustration.

The world of desire is characterized by the absence of fixed limits, for we can desire anything we can think of as good, however dimly we can imagine it. The world of limits, however, has quite different characteristics. One of its aspects is that certain things cannot be changed and must be accepted. One is born into a particular family in particular circumstances and at a given period in history without being previously consulted on any of these points. The world of limits tends to narrow with the passage of time, in the sense that limits encroach more and more, and possibilities that were once open become closed. This narrowing finally comes to a point in the experience of illness or old age, and of death.

Our decision necessarily involves an encounter with limits, in the sense that every decision is an act of self-limitation. Every decision contributes to the definition of the world of limits; it means an acceptance of one's basic limitation. Thus, in decision desire strains against limits, but limits continue to exist in some form,

---

[13] I am indebted to Bartholomew M. Kiely for his hypothesis on the tension between these two worlds in his book *Psychology and Moral Theology* (Rome: Gregorian University Press, 1980) 173–84, 199, 276.

and the fulfillment of desire is bounded by them; and, finally, there is the fact of death to be confronted.

Desire itself is not to be seen as *the* problem, so that the tension between desire and limits should be resolved by eliminating desire. The friends of God in the Bible are filled with the tumult and conflict of every form of desire. Desire is essential and ineradicable. If desire is recognized as essential and ineradicable, and limits equally so, then a tension between the world of desire and the world of limits must be seen as inevitable. The tension between desire and limitation is painful. It seems impossible to evade this tension altogether, since it is practically impossible that we should be altogether indifferent to the fulfillment of desire. There arises a practical exigence to treat something as if it were of absolute value; to make of something a guarantee of importance and well-being in the present and future. This means a distortion of reality if a finite good is involved. The distortion involved in creating the idol leads to further distortions of reality as one attempts to escape from limitation; and these distortions are generally attempted at the expense of others, as well as at the expense of the truth of one's own existence. In this sense one may understand, at least partly, the link between idolatry and other evils which is presented in Wisdom 14:22-29 and Romans 1:18-25: human relationships become violent and cruel rather than harmonious; there is a breakdown of fidelity between people and of respect for the truth in general.

The basic temptation to short-circuit the tension between desire and limitation is to try to make oneself the guarantee of one's own well-being and security. The basic temptation does not consist in the desire for morally reprehensible objects or activities whose appeal lies in their own immediate attraction. It consists rather in the desire to use such objects of desire (bad *or* good in themselves) as idols, in order to set oneself up as the guarantor of one's present and future well-being, to overcome by oneself and for oneself the fear of mortality; in brief, to make oneself God.

Just as the human body cannot survive without supplies from its environment, so the human person cannot survive without something beyond itself. The self-defensive concerns of the human person are rooted in the tension between desire and limits; they derive from the threats posed by the hazards of life and the fact of death.

We are not self-sufficient; we are not the master of our destiny. We experience the precariousness of our lives. We cannot ultimately be indifferent to our fate. We cannot live without some ground for our faith and hope, without basic trust, without some basic conviction about our own worth and well-being in the present and in the future. If this is true, it means that there is no human life that can be entirely neutral from a religious point of view: what grounds our basic faith and hope, in biblical terms, is either God or an idol.

All idolatry is implicitly self-idolatry, a making of ourselves into a god, refusing to transcend ourselves in allegiance to the transcendent reality of the Supreme Good that is God alone. The worshiper of idols attempts to manipulate God, to make God serve his or her purposes. (In Oriental thought the worship of an image was believed to give the idolater a power over the divinity represented; consequently, the Old Testament prohibited images of God.)[14] Idolatry represents the divinizing of created realities in the service of self-divinization. It represents a self-protective pseudo-solution in the attempt to cope with the problem of evil.

As to the possible objects of idolatry, the New Testament presents an extensive list: money (Matt 6:24), wine (Titus 2:3), the desire to dominate others (Col 3:5; Eph 5:5), political power (Acts 13:8), pleasure, envy, hate (Rom 6:19, Titus 3:3), and even the merely material observance of the Law (Gal 4:8). Idolatry in the New Testament signifies obsession with created things instead of total devotion to their Creator (e.g., Eph 5:5; Phil 3:19). It can take the form of moral narcissism as described in Luke's account of the Pharisee (18:9-17). Moral narcissism can express itself as legalism; in which case the concern with "rectitude" is the expression of the urge to self-justification rather than of theocentric self-transcendence. Every temptation seems to have an aspect of idolatry. Letting God be God involves a tension between desire and limits that is necessarily difficult for anyone to endure and overcome. The hope that comes from God's revelation in the words, deeds, and suffering of Christ cannot be a hope of evading the mystery of the Cross.

---

[14] Aidan Nichols, *The Art of God Incarnate* (London: Darton, Longman & Todd, 1980) 13–24.

This point is obvious in the extreme; for the Christian it is enough to establish that, whatever precise form the solution to this tension may take, it cannot mean an elimination of the problem. The temptations of Christ himself, as described in the Synoptic Gospels, may be interpreted in a related fashion: as specifically messianic temptations, yet as temptations to evade the conditions of limitation under which the messianic task was to be carried out.

If the human thrust to self-transcendence, which begins with the desire to know and extends to the desire to live responsibly, is to be brought to its fulfillment, there must be the hope of knowing Someone who transcends ourselves. If our willingness to know the truth (often unpleasant) and to accept responsibility and limitation (often difficult) is not to succumb to despair, then it must find an adequate source of freedom from the temptation to self-protection and pseudo-solutions to the problems of life and death.

In religious conversion a person no longer stands at the center of his or her own world in terms of what he or she knows, hopes for, and loves. Religious faith, hope, and love derive from the love with which God floods our hearts through the Holy Spirit he has given us (Rom 5:5). God is the loving source of our religious faith and hope and love through which we intend God in all our intending. The Christian tradition makes explicit our implicit intending of God in all our intending by speaking of the Holy Spirit that God has given to us. Through the gift of God's love, we must find our center beyond ourselves, surrendering ourselves to God in faith, hope, and charity, and leaving it to God to effect an ultimate solution to the tension between desire and limitation in our lives.

Faith, the knowledge born of love, is the apprehension of transcendent value, in whose light all other values are relativized. In the light of faith the divine love and light is the originating value of all created values, linking itself to all other values, transforming, transfiguring, magnifying, and glorifying them. As Augustine remarked, "in every man who is converted to God his delight is changed, his pleasures are changed (not taken away, but changed)."[15] With the hope born of religious love, the limit of human experience

---

[15] St. Augustine, *In Psalmos* 74 n 1, PL 36, 946; *Corpus Christianorum Series Latina XXXIX,* p. 1024.

ceases to be the grave.[16] Hope is the security and confidence of those to whom God has given God's love. It liberates us both from despair as regards the fulfillment of our deepest desire and from the presumption of wishing to be the guarantor of our own fulfillment. God is love, says St. John (1 John 4:8, 16), and that love overflows in creative and redemptive activity. So, too, the gift of God's love, the creation and communication of that love in our hearts, overflows into the love of our neighbor. "There is nothing which so draws us to return love," wrote Chrysostom, "as when we understand that he who loves us is urgently longing for our affection."[17] God's love floods our hearts and calls for our response; the gift of God's Holy Spirit, the gift of Love Proceeding, is graciously at work whenever we respond to God with an authentically self-transcending love for others.

Jesus Christ, the light of the world (John 9:5), has given us his radiant Spirit to lead us through the darkness (John 19:30; 20:22). It is the Spirit of his love that enabled him to endure his suffering and death for our salvation (Phil 2:5-11). The Spirit of his love and hope makes endurable what otherwise would be meaningless and unendurable (e.g., Heb 12:2). It both enables and calls for our sharing Christ's life of self-giving love in his Way of the Cross, the only way to Happiness Itself (God); for the Spirit of Christ is the Spirit of Happiness Itself radiant in the darkness of the human condition, illuminating our way to Happiness Itself. Both the eye of love that is Christian faith and the look of love that is Christian contemplation evidence the way that Christ has given sight to the blind through the gift of his radiant Spirit of self-giving love. It enables us to share the Father's vision of his Beloved Son (Mark 1:11; 9:7), the vision of our hope and joy; for the loving Father sees in the darkness what unlove cannot hope to see. The radiance of the Father's Spirit enables us both to recognize and to enjoy this beauty of self-giving love in the Beloved Son.

The following chapters examine the tensional symbolism of biblical narratives for insight into the mystery of the Cross as the

---

[16] Lonergan, *Method in Theology,* 116.
[17] St. John Chrysostom, *Hom.* 14.1-2, *PG* 61, 497–99.

way that God chose to act in human history, in "a Christ who is the power and wisdom of God" (1 Cor 1:23-24).

The encounter with God as revealed in Jesus Christ is the basic reality which makes a total claim on us. Our response to this total claim, our letting ourselves be lead by Christ's radiant Spirit, corresponds to Bernard Lonergan's idea of religious conversion.

The gift of God, in the self-giving act of revelation, calls for our corresponding self-giving. This self-giving is expressed in certain basic attitudes which are at the same time the challenge and the gift of God. These basic attitudes seek practical expression on the level of norms of action which are the product of intellectual reflection, taking place within an anthropological context basically defined by the fact of revelation in Jesus Christ. As human beings we cannot resolve the basic problem of reconciling desire and limitation, life and death. The problem can only be solved by God's making a gift of new possibilities. God's startling revelation of God's love for us in the words and deeds of Jesus Christ is for the community of Christian faith the compelling solution to the problem.

Human desire can be only partially fulfilled in this life. There always remains a residue of nonfulfillment and difficulty. In the face of this situation of partial fulfillment, two quite different attitudes are possible. One might focus one's attention on the area of nonfulfillment in a state of constant resentment; and the most sure way to be unhappy is to make one's happiness dependent on the fulfillment of impossible conditions. But a radically different attitude is also possible. The possibility of enjoying anything at all must be based on a kind of humility that takes nothing for granted but lives in a continual state of surprise. Humility brings an appreciation of everything, and especially of people, even when they are superficially unattractive. The central idea of humility is gratitude, and the foundation of both humility and gratitude is the dogma of creation: we have no absolute right either to have things to enjoy, or to exist ourselves; both are unmerited gifts. Until we realize that things might not be, we cannot appreciate that things are. Pride would take things for granted, and clamor for more, in continual dissatisfaction; thus destroying everything, including happiness; but humility keeps wonder alive. Here there is involved a radical acceptance of limitation, the acceptance of the fact that one need not have existed.

But if the world, and one's own existence, are accepted in gratitude, that does not mean passivity. If the world is good, it deserves to be improved. This implies no naive faith in inevitable success; on the contrary. Such basic commitment, like appreciation, takes nothing for granted, and least of all success. Acceptance of the world in wonder and gratitude grounds a strenuous desire to improve the world.

Yet, if one does not bargain on success, success too may be received as a gift; more precisely, as grace. One does not presume on one's own merits; but one dares to hope for and to strive for unmerited successes (cf. Luke 1:46-55 and Ephesians 3:7-12).

It is a radical acceptance of limits which takes nothing for granted (in the sense of ceasing to be surprised and grateful for everything and anything) which makes happiness possible. We have many needs which must be to some degree met if we are to survive and develop; so we are inevitably concerned with ourselves to some extent. Here there is a continual possibility of some kind of narcissistic self-involvement. Humility and gratitude can convert such needs from occasions of narcissism into occasions of self-transcendence; and the contingency of so much of life, from being an intolerable threat, becomes the source of wonder.

The Paradigm:
Jesus, Religious Authorities, Disciples[18]

The symbolic gospel narratives disclose the tensional structure of Christian life within the pulls and counterpulls (dialectical differences) between the ways of God and the ways of humanity without God. Jesus, the protagonist, expresses the ways of God; the religious authorities, his antagonists, express the ways of humanity without God. The disciples appear to be of two minds and hence inwardly divided. On the one hand, they are the followers of Jesus and the ways of God. On the other hand, they fail at

---

[18] Jack Dean Kingsbury employs this paradigm in *Conflict in Mark* and *Conflict in Luke* (Minneapolis: Fortress Press, 1989 and 1991).

critical times to demonstrate the kind of spiritual maturity that Jesus expects of them. Their double-mindedness is most manifest in Peter, who despite repenting afterwards, denies Jesus (Luke 22:54-62).

The disciples express the tensional structure of Christian life within the pulls and counterpulls (dialectical differences) between the ways of God and the ways of humanity. They share the traits of Jesus in their spiritual maturity; they display the traits of the religious authorities in their spiritual waywardness. Finally, the crucified and risen Christ will bring them to spiritual maturity. And it is a mark of this maturity, in Luke's Gospel story (24:52), that "they worship him as he ascends to heaven." This act of worship expresses the ultimate hope of the Christian community in every age that the crucified and risen Christ will bring them to spiritual maturity through the Spirit that has been poured out upon them.

The following chapters examine the relationship between our symbolic gospel narratives and the tensional structure of Christian life in our Spirit-guided quest for the fullness of life in the kingdom.

Excursus:
Religious Consciousness and the Language of Interiority

For Lonergan the same general structure of intentional consciousness is shared by all human beings. As such, and in contrast to any particular content of that consciousness, it crosses all particular cultures and times. The specific articulation of this general structure will vary both within and across cultures, but the reality of consciousness itself will not. Lonergan describes this structure in terms of a number of discrete levels of consciousness, each of which can in principle be attended to and verified as operative within the consciousness of any individual.

Typically, Lonergan speaks about four levels of consciousness: empirical consciousness, through which we sense, imagine, feel and move; intellectual consciousness, through which we question, gain understanding and express our understandings; rational consciousness, through which we weigh evidence and assess the truth, falsity and probability of our understandings; and responsible consciousness, through which we deliberate, evaluate, decide and act.[19] Sometimes, Lonergan speaks of a "fifth level of consciousness," the level of religious and mystical consciousness.[20]

All these levels of consciousness are intrinsically linked to each other along a spectrum of expanding "subjectivity" or the expanding functioning of a drive toward knowledge, value and self-transcendence.[21] This drive can be further specified by attending to and verifying a norm operative on and inherent within each level. On the level of empirical consciousness, the norm is "Be attentive!"; for intellectual consciousness, "Be intelligent!"; for rational consciousness, "Be critical!"; for responsible consciousness, "Be responsible!"; for religious consciousness, "Be loving!"[22]

The first moment of religious consciousness, for Lonergan is one of vital intersubjectivity. In vital intersubjectivity, there is no object; the union is one of two subjects as subjects. It is not by sharing a common object, but by sharing a common consciousness that they are united. Intersubjectivity becomes aware of itself through a heightened attention to the subject as intersubjective. The subject experiences one's self and one's acts as united to the self and acts of another. One has a direct and immediate experience of relationship. One must distinguish between consciousness and attention; for one may be consciously in love with another for some time before a belated attentiveness brings it into awareness.

Once attended to, one's love (intersubjective relation) can then become the object of intellectual inquiry; one can seek to understand it, to judge it and to make decisions on the basis of it. The intellectual process of coming to know love is different from the intersubjective experience of it.

The first moment of religious consciousness is a moment of religious (mystical) intersubjectivity. It is not the experience of an object but a shared consciousness, a vital union with a consciousness that transcends the human. "God's gift of God's love," when

---

[19] Bernard Lonergan, *Method in Theology,* 2nd ed. (New York: Herder & Herder, 1972) 9.

[20] Ibid., 105, 107, 109.

[21] Lonergan, *Second Collection,* 73, 80.

[22] Lonergan, *Method,* 53.

transposed into the categories of interiority and correlated with the structures of human consciousness, refers not to the experience of an object, but to the vital union of an individual's consciousness-as-consciousness with the transcendent consciousness-as-consciousness. In religious (mystical) consciousness the experience is one of the subject as transcendently intersubjective. In Lonergan's terms, one becomes conscious of "a clouded revelation of absolute intelligence and intelligibility, absolute truth and reality, absolute goodness and holiness?"[23] There is no question of an object in this vital intersubjective union. It is consciousness, not knowledge, and as such is the experience of mystery.[24]

* * *

Happiness Itself/God is self-communicating in giving us the Spirit of Happiness Itself which enables both our vision (the eye and look of love/faith and contemplation) and our enjoyment of our relational existence (self–others–world–God) in communion with Happiness Itself. The grace/gift (Spirit of Happiness Itself) of Happiness Itself enables us to participate in the cognitive and affective life of Happiness Itself: the enjoyment of the beauty and goodness and truth/reality of Happiness Itself as our Origin and Ground and Destiny. The Spirit of Happiness Itself "descends" (Incarnation and Pentecost) that we might "ascend" into the realm of Happiness Itself. We are the created effects of the uncreated Cause that is Happiness Itself/God whose will for us is always Happiness Itself. Our hunger and thirst or desire for happiness, the dynamic structure of human intentionality, is not of our own making; rather, it evidences that we have been structured or preprogrammed by Happiness Itself for Happiness Itself. Our basic faith

---

[23] Lonergan, *Method,* 116.
[24] Lonergan, *Method,* 106. St. Gertrude (d. 1302), a Benedictine nun and most important German medieval mystic, experienced such a vital intersubjective union with God that even when eating an apple she was conscious of God's enjoying it with her. As the created effect of an uncreated Creator's consciously knowing and loving and enjoying what he is "effecting," St. Gertrude's consciousness is a shared consciousness or vital union with her transcendent Creator's consciousness.

in the reality of Happiness Itself leads us to seek educators of that faith which might lead us to Happiness Itself. Jesus Christ, the educator of Christian faith, affirms that he is the Way of Happiness Itself, the Truth/Reality of Happiness Itself, and the Life of Happiness Itself as the grace/self-gift and call of Happiness Itself for all humankind.

Scriptural (written word) iconography (image) corresponds to the Word/Meaning and Perfect Image of God that is Jesus Christ. The iconographer "writes" the sacred image because it communicates the Word of God Incarnate. Because we cannot do what we cannot, at least in some way imagine, we need an image for a God who is the credible object of our believing, the trustworthy object of our hoping, and the worthy object of our loving. As the "perfect image of God," Jesus enables Christian faith, hope, and love. As the Incarnate Word of God, Jesus Christ communicates the true meaning of our relationship to God in Christian faith, hope, and love.

Sacred Scriptures were not written for our "reading"; rather, they were written for our prayerful contemplation with the "eye of love" that is religious faith and the "look of love" that is religious contemplation delighting in what it contemplates. The written story that is the Christian Scripture communicates the life story of the crucified and risen Christ to the prayerful Christian "reader" who enjoys the gift of Christ's Spirit, enabling the Christian contemplation of the risen Christ. The sacred Christian icons serve the same purpose, fostering the Christian community's communion and communication with its crucified and risen Lord.

The triad of death–Satan–sin represents all that is contrary to or the absence of Happiness Itself. The beauty of Happiness Itself brings form to the deformed, integration to the disintegrated, cosmos to chaos, the harmony of peace to the disharmony of conflict, the enjoyment of community, communion and communication to the alienated.

1

Mark: Transfigured or Disfigured?

Although the Israelites spoke of God in human terms, they always remembered the difference between God and human beings: "I am God and not man" (Hos 11:9). Isaiah expresses the irreducible difference in terms of flesh and spirit (31:3). Israel understood that it was impossible to reduce God to the human level or to define a reality as mysterious and yet as manifest as life itself.

"God alone is good" (Mark 10:18)

The human ego is not the ultimate context of all human life, despite our futile attempts to act as if it were. The pedagogy of the Christian community and its New Testament writers assumes that true love means loving others as they truly are: "God alone is good" (Mark 10:18); therefore, "Love the Lord your God with all your heart, with all your soul, with all your mind, and with all your strength" (Mark 12:29-30); secondly, "Love your neighbor as yourself" (Mark 12:31). Only when we love God above all do we experience the joy of loving God as God truly is. We frustrate ourselves in attempting to love God for less than he is, for no other is absolutely lovable. No other can satisfy the human heart. We also frustrate ourselves when we attempt to love ourselves above all; for we are not absolutely lovable. The deification of loved persons puts an impossible burden on human relationships. Self-idolatry precludes the joy of truly loving the limited, finite, relational persons that we are both in ourselves and in all other human persons.

Throughout the New Testament Jesus rejoices in loving others as they truly are. Without reserve he gives all to God (Luke 23:46). He gives his life for his friends to bring them the joy of his love for his absolutely and perfectly lovable Father, no less than the joy of his Father's love for him (John 15:9-15). To share his joy, we must love the Father as the Father truly is. To share the Father's joy, we must love the Son as he truly is (John 8:42; 14:21-24): one with the Father. Jesus Christ enables us to love as he loved by giving us his Spirit and his mother (Rom 5:5; John 10:27), uniting us with God as he truly is and with one another as we truly are in the body of Christ and the temple of his Spirit. The joy that accompanies such love is the fruit of the Spirit (Gal 5:22) and evidence of the kingdom of God (Rom 14:17). The love by which the faithful are united in the truth (1 Cor 13:6) brings an enduring joy which inspires prayer and unceasing thanksgiving (1 Thess 5:16; Phil 3:1; 4:1-6).

"You think not the things of God, but human things" (Mark 8:33)

Jesus, the protagonist of Mark's Gospel, views reality—what is good or bad, right or wrong, true or false—the way God does.[1] He knows and loves God and humankind as they truly are. He is supremely the one who "thinks the things of God" (Mark 8:33), viewing reality as God would have us view it, and not in this-worldly terms. His authority derives from his unique relationship to God his Father. He is the Beloved Son of God (Mark 1:11; 9:7; 12:6). The religious authorities in Mark's story are the antagonists of Jesus. They "think the things of humans" instead of "the things of God" (Mark 8:33). It is their viewing reality from a merely human standpoint instead of from God's standpoint that puts them on the side of Satan in the cosmic struggle between God and Satan. God is at work in Jesus to defeat Satan and his minions and to summon humankind to repent, to think and love and act as the friends of God, and to live in the sphere of his end-time rule of peace.

---

[1] Jack Dean Kingsbury, *Conflict in Mark* (Minneapolis: Fortress Press, 1989) 4–8.

In the course of Mark's story, Jesus exhibits, by what he says and does or what is narrated of him, a multiplicity of character traits. Still, all of Jesus' character traits ultimately spring from the fact that he is uniquely related to God his Father (1:11; 9:7; 12:16). By virtue of this unique relationship, Jesus is who he is, the Son of God, and his mission accomplishes salvation for all humankind (Mark 14:24).

Relative to his mission, Jesus is authoritative (1:10). Empowered by God's Spirit, Jesus withstands the testing of Satan, preaches the gospel of God's end-time rule, calls disciples, teaches God's will, heals the sick, exorcises demons, bests his opponents in debate, and goes the Way of the Cross. Jesus, the Son of God, is decisively God's supreme agent, God's "Good News" in whom his end-time rule has drawn near to save and transform all humankind. Toward God, Jesus is "whole," for he loves God with heart, soul, mind, and strength (12:29-30). Manifesting and communicating God's rule, Jesus loves God with all his heart, for he is perfectly obedient to God (1:12-13). Jesus loves God with all his soul, for in doing God's will he does not withhold even the giving of his life (14:36; 15:37). And Jesus loves God with all his mind and strength, for he lays no claim for himself to either the prerogatives of worldly power or the security of home, family, and possessions (1:38-39; 3:31-35; 10:21, 42-45). Toward himself, Jesus has the integrity of one in whom there is no discrepancy between what he says and what he does. Jesus' teaching is embodied in his behavior, and his behavior attests to the truth of his teaching (e.g., Mark 8:34-35; 15:24-37). Toward his disciples, Jesus is enabling and loyal. He shares his life with his disciples. In calling his disciples, Jesus empowers them to leave behind their former way of life and to follow him and be with him (e.g., Mark 1:17-18, 20; 2:14; 3:13-16; 10:28). Although he knows that they will betray, forsake, and deny him, he also graciously promises them that he will reconcile them to himself (cf. Mark 14:18, 27, 30; 16:7). Toward the crowd and individuals of faith, Jesus is compassionate. He has compassion for the crowd; he recognizes that they are leaderless, like sheep without a shepherd (6:34). Similarly, he heals the afflicted when they, or others on their behalf, appeal to him in trust that he can restore them (1:40-42; 9:21-27).

Jesus' self-giving death manifests both the wholeness of his love for God and his compassion for all humankind. He serves all others (10:42-45) in giving his life to establish the new covenant community and atone for the sins of all (14:24; 15:38). He reveals that true love for others is not lording over them but compassionately serving them (10:42-45).

Jesus clashes with the religious authorities when they refuse the summons of both John and himself to repent and when they see in him the agent of Satan instead of the agent of God (1:14-15; 3:22, 30). Even his confrontations with the religious authorities are a form of service; for he summons them to think the things of God and to enter into the sphere of God's peace and joy. His confrontational love is always for the deliverance and the salvation of his adversaries.

Traits of the Disciples

If Jesus, the protagonist of Mark's story, always "thinks the things of God," and the religious authorities, the antagonists, "think the things not of God, but of humans" (8:33), the disciples possess conflicting traits.[2] Initially, Mark casts them as loyal, committed, authoritative, enlightened, and supportive. Despite their promising beginning, the disciples progressively evince a human, this-worldly perspective in most of what they say and do. They seem ever more prone to "think the things of humans." There is conflict between them and Jesus, for at issue is the meaning of discipleship.

Mark discloses the character traits of the disciples primarily through their interaction with Jesus. If the many traits Jesus exhibits spring from one root trait, the many traits that the disciples exhibit spring from two conflicting traits. The disciples are at once loyal and uncomprehending. They are loyal: Jesus summons them to follow him and they immediately leave behind their former way of life and give him their total allegiance (e.g., 1:16-20; 3:13-16; 10:28). They are also uncomprehending: they do not fully understand the identity of Jesus and, therefore, the essential meaning of discipleship. They consequently forsake him during his passion.

---

[2] Jack Dean Kingsbury, *Conflict in Mark,* 8. See chapter 4, "The Story of the Disciples," 89–117.

Initially, Mark casts the disciples as loyal, committed, and authoritative, for Jesus imparts to them authority and they enthusiastically embrace Jesus' ministry to Israel. They preach, teach, heal, and exorcise demons (3:14-15; 6:7, 12-13, 15, 30). The disciples are observant, for they remain with Jesus, bearing witness to what he says and does (3:14). The disciples are obedient, for Jesus commands and they comply (e.g., 1:38; 3:9, 13; 4:1, 35-36; 6:7-8, 12-13, 31-32, 38, 41, 45; 8:1, 6-7). The disciples are enlightened, for God discloses to them the mystery of the kingdom (4:11) and Jesus explains to them the meaning of his parables (4:34). The disciples are supportive, for although Jesus must defend them in controversy, they nonetheless stand at his side (e.g., 2:15-16, 18, 23-24; 7:1-5). The disciples are vulnerable, for they risk attack by the religious authorities precisely because they follow Jesus (e.g., 2:18-20; 7:1-2, 5).

Interlaced with the favorable traits of the disciples are also conflicting, negative traits. Because they are uncomprehending either in mind or heart or both, they reveal themselves, in the middle of Mark's story, to be cowardly, bereft of faith, fearful, distraught, groundlessly astonished, and hard of heart.

Although enlightened by God, who gives them the mystery of the kingdom, the disciples do not, as Jesus expects, understand his parables (4:13; 7:17-18). Moreover, in three boat scenes and two feeding miracles they further evince a lack of understanding. In the first boat scene, the disciples show that they have not perceived who Jesus is (4:41). Far from resting secure in his sustaining presence when threatened by a storm, they prove themselves to be cowardly, bereft of faith, and fearful (4:40-41). In the two feeding miracles, the disciples, though endowed by Jesus with authority, nonetheless become distraught and treat as fantasy Jesus' calling for them to feed the five thousand (6:35-37) and the four thousand (8:2-4). In the second boat scene, the disciples, having now witnessed Jesus himself feed the five thousand, still demonstrate their inability to comprehend either the dimensions of his divine authority or that they can rest secure in his sustaining presence. Encountering a heavy wind and seeing Jesus walk on water, they think him to be a ghost and, becoming fearful they cry aloud in terror (6:48-50); and after Jesus has caused the wind to abate, they are, for sheer lack of comprehension, astonished at his feat (6:51-52). And in the second and third boat scenes, the disciples have seen Jesus feed the five thousand prior to the one scene and both the five thousand and the four thousand prior to the other; yet it is because they fail to completely grasp the reality that Jesus can meet any need that both Mark as narrator and Jesus castigate them as "hard of heart" (6:52; 8:17-21).

In the end section of Mark's story (8:27–16:8), the disciples become ever more uncomprehending, until they at last fall away from Jesus. In situations calling for faith, trust, insight, confession and action, they tend to fail seriously in one respect or another. They remain loyal until Jesus' arrest at Gethsemane (14:50). They still follow Jesus and exhibit positive character traits. They continue to be witnesses to Jesus' words and deeds (e.g., 14:22). They are obedient, as when Jesus twice sends two of them either to fetch a colt on which he rides into Jerusalem (10:1-7) or to make preparations for celebrating the Passover meal (14:13-16).

Throughout the end section of Mark's story, the disciples do not understand Jesus' ministry of suffering and death (8:31). They are unable to grasp the nature of discipleship, which has its focus in service and not in self-concern (8:34-35). Their incomprehension gives rise to the negative traits that the disciples display in the end of Mark's story.

On the way to Jerusalem, the disciples are three times unreceptive to Jesus' passion predictions that the purpose of his ministry is to suffer and die (8:31; 9:31; 10:33). Following Jesus' first passion prediction, Peter manifests his incomprehension by rebuking Jesus (8:32-33). At the mount of transfiguration, Peter, James, and John do not grasp the revelation and are overcome by fright (9:5-6). The disciples left below, though they have the authority to cast out demons (3:15; 6:7), do not avail themselves of this authority and hence are ineffectual in their attempt to heal the boy with the unclean spirit (9:14-29).

After Jesus' second passion prediction, the failure of the disciples to grasp the meaning of Jesus' ministry appears in their various attitudes. They are status-conscious, for they quarrel over who among them is the greatest (9:34) and they attempt to turn away those bringing children to Jesus for blessing (9:13-14). They are exclusive, for they would forbid one who is not a member of their circle from exorcising demons in Jesus' name (9:38-40). They are enamored of wealth, for they espouse the conventional wisdom that sees in wealth a sign of God's special favor (10:23-27). And they are anxious about the future, for Peter demands to know of Jesus what they, who have left all to follow him, can anticipate the future will hold for them (10:23-31).

No sooner has Jesus uttered his third passion prediction than James and John, desirous of power and position, approach him requesting for themselves the places of greatest honor in his glory (10:35-40). The ten take offense at this, not because their motives are purer, but because they desire these places for themselves (10:41).

Once Jesus has reached Jerusalem and entered on his passion, the disciples' incomprehension manifests itself in new ways. In the house of Simon the leper, they are seemingly among those indignantly scolding the woman who has poured expensive ointment on the head of Jesus (14:3-9). They miss the meaning of her act. Jesus rebukes them for their failure to understand that she has done "a beautiful thing" to him (14:6). She has anointed his body for burial (14:8). At the Last Supper, Judas discloses that he is at heart deceitful. Together with the other disciples, he asks Jesus whether he will be the one to betray him in such a manner as to anticipate that Jesus' answer will be negative (14:19). At the Mount of Olives and at Gethsemane, the disciples stand out as self-deluded. At the Mount of Olives, Peter, joined by the others, insists that he will die with Jesus rather than deny him (14:31). At Gethsemane, however, Peter, James, and John put the lie to the confidence they just expressed. Far from suffering death with Jesus, they cannot summon the strength even to watch with him for an hour but instead fall asleep (14:37, 40-41). Finally, the consequences of the disciples' incomprehension becomes manifest with Judas' betrayal of Jesus (14:43-46), the disciples flight (14:50), and Peter's denial of Jesus (14:54, 66-72).

Mark's last word about the disciples is not one of disloyalty but of promise. Even when predicting that the disciples will fall away from him, Jesus pledges that after he has been raised, he will go before them into Galilee where, the young man in white at the tomb adds, they will see him (14:28; 16:7). Mark leads his readers to think of the disciples as reconciled followers of Jesus and not as apostates. The crucified and risen Christ will make good his pledge to his disciples, ultimately enabling them to think and to enjoy the things of God above all, to apprehend all reality in the light and shadow of God. In the shadow, for God is supreme and incomparable. In the light, for God originates, sustains, transforms, magnifies, and glorifies all reality within God's all-encompassing goodness.

Traits of the Religious Authorities

The antagonists of Jesus in Mark's story are the religious authorities.[3] They are the rulers in Israel, entrusted by God with the care of Israel. They see Jesus as a mortal threat to both themselves and the people. They form a united front against Jesus.

Just as the many character traits of Jesus stem from one root trait (being uniquely related to God), so the many character traits of the authorities stem from one root trait. They are without divine authority (1:22); therefore, they "think the things of humans" instead of "the things of God" (8:33). They are, in fact, on the side of Satan, the Adversary of God (8:33).

The religious authorities in Mark's story are Israel's leaders (e.g., 12:2; 14:1-2; 15:1). Like the disciples, they make their debut in the middle of the story (1:14-8:26), after Jesus has began his ministry. Even before they have had the opportunity to speak or to act, they are described as being "without authority" (1:22): they view things from a purely human viewpoint instead of from God's viewpoint. Their character traits attest to this.

The religious authorities are hypocritical in their practice of religion in relation to both God and the people. There is a discrepancy between appearance and underlying truth (7:6-7; 12:14-15, 38-40). While ostensibly they teach God's word and will, in reality they teach the commandments of men (7:6-7). They are hypo-

---

[3] Jack Dean Kingsbury, *Conflict in Mark,* 14. See chapter 3, "The Story of the Authorities," 63–88.

critical toward the people, for their religiosity masks a desire that great deference and honor be paid to them (12:38-40). They perceive themselves to be righteous (2:17). They identify God's will with themselves: they are the ones who know and do it.

The religious authorities are false teachers (12:24, 27). Mark stresses that they are in error by having the "friendly scribe" who is himself one of the authorities, pay tribute to Jesus' superior knowledge of the Law (12:28, 32-33). Although the religious authorities esteem themselves to be expert in matters of Scripture and therefore of the Law and religion, Jesus shows that they are unable to understand the true meaning of Scripture. Jesus charges that they do not know Scripture (12:24). Scripture predicts that Elijah will come and restore all things, but the authorities are blind to the fact that Elijah has already appeared in the person of John the Baptist and they have repudiated him (9:11-13; 11:31). Scripture also says that Jesus himself must suffer and be rejected, but the insight that the way the authorities have treated John presages the way they will treat Jesus has eluded them (9:12-13). And if the Scripture tells the authorities that the Messiah is the Son of David, the fact that it likewise tells them that the Messiah is more than the Son of David (and is indeed the Son of God) escapes them (12:35-37).

The religious authorities misinterpret Scripture to make it serve their own purposes. Although Mosaic Law commands that parents be honored, the religious authorities allow children to nullify this command by denying their parents the support they are otherwise obligated to give them (7:10-13). Although Mosaic Law reveals that God's intention at creation was that divorce not be permitted, the religious authorities appeal to the concession Moses made to the hardness of the human heart in order to justify divorce (10:2-9). And although the book of Moses attests to the resurrection of the dead, the Sadducees deny there is any such thing (12:18-27). Instead of honoring God's command that his house be a place of prayer for all the nations, the chief priests have turned the Temple into their own sacrilegious preserve (11:17). While claiming to teach God's word, they promulgate instead their own doctrines as embodied in the tradition of the elders (7:6-13).

The religious authorities are also hard of heart, loveless, and legalistic. When Jesus does good on the Sabbath and heals the man with the withered hand, the religious leaders do not rejoice but instead find in this an infraction of the Sabbath law. They turn the Sabbath into the day they themselves do evil and conspire how to destroy Jesus (3:1-6). In point of fact, the "friendly scribe" notes the basic difference separating Jesus and the religious authorities in terms of what it is to do the will of God. Whereas the essential matter for Jesus is loving God and neighbor, for the authorities it is strict adherence to Law and tradition as they define this.

When Mark has the "friendly scribe" say that love of God and neighbor are to take precedence over all burnt offerings and sacrifices (12:32-33), Mark is in effect using the friendly scribe to identify the two contrasting positions of Jesus and the religious authorities on doing the will of God. Doing God's will for Jesus is always a form of exercising God's love. God's will for us is always God's love for us. For the religious authorities, doing God's will consists of attending to the letter of the Law and tradition as defined by them. They are religious formalists devoid of an authentically religious spirit.

The religious authorities are implacably opposed to Jesus from the start (2:1–3:6). They regard him as the agent of Satan (3:22) who, because of his alleged assault on Law (2:23-28; 3:1-5), tradition (2:15-17, 18-20; 7:1-13), and Temple (11:15-18; 14:56-58), threatens their overthrow as Israel's leaders (11:15-18; 12:1-12) and Israel's ruin.

The numerous traits of the religious authorities spring from their implacable opposition to Jesus. Like Satan, they repeatedly put Jesus to the test. They call upon him to prove that he acts on the authority of God and not Satan by specifying a sign that God is to perform in their sight (8:11-13). Aware of Jesus' stand against divorce, they challenge Jesus to prove that he does not teach counter to Moses' permission of divorce (10:2-9). They attempt to entice Jesus to say whether the Law sanctions paying the poll tax to Caesar. They are hypocritical in giving the appearance of requesting honest information from him, whereas they are seeking to entrap him (12:13-17). The authorities are conspiratorial in their conflict with Jesus. Four times they take counsel against

Jesus either on how to destroy him (3:6; 11:18) or to arrest him (12:12) or both (14:1) without stirring up the crowd (11:18; 12:12; 14:1-2) or on how to proceed in delivering him to Pilate (15:1). They are deceitful and cunning in bringing about the arrest and death of Jesus (14:1). They eagerly accept Judas' offer to betray Jesus and promise him money (14:10-11). They manipulate the crowd who heard Jesus with delight as he daily taught in the Temple to arrest him (12:37; 14:43, 48-49). At Jesus' trial, they unsuccessfully attempt to get Jesus sentenced to death on the basis of false testimony (14:55-60). And before Pilate, they falsely accuse Jesus, after he affirms that he is the King of the Jews, of sedition against Rome, in the face of which Jesus remains silent (15:2-5). They are envious of Jesus (15:10). Their hostility towards Jesus at his hearing before Pilate convinces Pilate that they act out of envy (15:1-5). They are blasphemous in accusing Jesus of blasphemy against God. Ironically, they blaspheme God in attacking Jesus, who is God's Son. When Jesus forgives the paralytic his sins, they charge him with blasphemy and thus deny him his God-given authority to grant forgiveness (2:6-7). Witnessing Jesus' exorcisms, they sin against God's Spirit by declaring that Jesus acts on the authority of Satan (3:22, 28-30). Their blasphemies continue both at Jesus' trial (14:61-64) and as Jesus hangs on the cross (15:2, 31-32).

The authorities are consistently accusatory in dealing with Jesus and his disciples. When the disciples pluck grain on the Sabbath (2:23-24), the authorities approach Jesus and charge them with breaking the Law. When they see the disciples eating with ritually unclean hands, they approach Jesus and demand to know why the disciples transgress the tradition of the elders (7:1-5).

The authorities are remiss as leaders of the people. Jesus looks out over the crowd and has compassion on them, for they are leaderless, as sheep without a shepherd (6:34). The authorities are faithless to their religious trust. They are pretentious and ostentatious in exploiting Israel's religious heritage for their own self-promotion. They desire to be seen, praised, and honored by the crowd. They walk about in special garments, accept deferential greetings in the marketplace, assume the best seats at banquets and in synagogues, and offer long prayers (12:38-40).

Thinking the things not of God, but of humans, always entails a form of self-idolatry, of attempting to substitute something for God, which precludes the joy of loving Happiness Itself (God). The traits of the religious authorities represent the obstacles within the human heart to our enjoyment of the Good News of Happiness Itself in Jesus Christ, the Son of God. The incapacity of the religious authorities to enjoy seems to be connected with their incapacity to love. They cannot enjoy anything enough to be able to forget about themselves. Their self-righteousness, self-importance, and self-absorption are aspects of their futile attempt to substitute the part for the whole, the self and the human for the self and the human together with their all-encompassing and all-fulfilling God. Such self-idolatry precludes the joy of our truly loving ourselves, others, and God as we truly are.

Conflicting Desires

The first thing that we read about God in the Bible is that he made something and affirmed its goodness/beauty. St. Thomas writes of the love of benevolence or friendship that by it the person who loves desires for the beloved the same goods that one desires for oneself as for another self. And so the lover desires to give the beloved the same things that are the objects of one's own love and enjoyment (*ST* I–II, q. 27, a. 3). Similarly, Mark's Jesus would share the joy and happiness of God with all humankind. Jesus' grace and call to the happiness of God meets with resistance among those who cannot, however implicitly, believe that God is always God's best gift. The unbeliever assumes there is something or someone better.

Mark's tightly woven narrative expresses the tensional structure of human life in terms of two contrasting ways of life competing for the human heart: that of "saving one's life out of fear," and that of "losing one's life for others out of faith" (8:35). David Rhoads presents the Markan view of the two ways as follows:[4]

---

[4] David Rhoads, "Losing Life for Others in the Face of Death: Mark's Standards of Judgment" in *Interpretation* XLVII (4) (1993) 359–60.

What People Want for Themselves	What God Wants for People
self-centered	other-centered
save one's own life	lose one's life for the Good News
acquire the world	give up possessions
lord over others	be servant of all
be anxious	have faith
fear	courage
harming others	saving others
loyalty to self	loyalty to God for the world

Mark's narrative consistently promotes the one way of life and condemns the other. Jesus embodies what God wills for people. His self-giving love is expressed when he heals, drives out demons, pardons sins, and dies for this mission. The religious authorities represent what people want in order to aggrandize themselves at the expense of others. The disciples vacillate between these two ways. They are torn between following Jesus in the service of the Good News (the self-giving love and life of Happiness Itself available in Jesus Christ) and seeking status, power, and a security of their own. Jesus' self-surrender to God, his Way of the Cross, clashes with the desire for self-sufficiency and self-aggrandizement. Jesus' freedom to love God above all is his freedom (*from* self-idolatry) *for* the service of all others in communion with God who loves all.

Living in God's Love

The three affirmations of Sonship around which Mark structures his narrative suggest a Markan model for the entire event and process of Christian conversion. The relationship of human persons to the Beloved Son moves from nonrecognition at Jesus' baptism (1:11) through incipient recognition at his Transfiguration (9:7) to full recognition at his death (14:24). Mark's readers will experience the goodness of God's affirming love in their lives only if they will allow themselves to be drawn to him along the Way of the Cross. In the self-gift of his Son, God wills to make us the locus of his own self-giving to all humankind. In the measure that we allow ourselves to be totally receptive to God we find our center outside our self. In that measure can God make us the fountain from which God's love will flow to others. Mark's Good News, the concrete goodness of his news, is the same news that Paul gave to the Corinthians: that "for our sake God made the sinless one into sin, so that in him we might become the goodness of God" (2 Cor 5:21).

Mark's narrative is an extended symbol of God's self-investment in his Son, the Beloved, a self-investing love that calls forth and creates love in all who receive the Spirit of the Son. Mark's Gospel summons each reader to hear the words of God: "You are my Son, the Beloved, in whom I delight" (1:11). Mark is engaged in the cognitive-affective transformation of his readers, a transformation that issues from the felt meaning of God's loving self-investment in their lives. Mark wants his readers to accept as the integrating center of their lives the Supreme and Beloved Goodness whose life has been poured out for them. Letting God be God means letting God invest in our lives the fulfilling goodness and joy of the Beloved Son and Spirit.

Mark's opening statement declares the purpose of his gospel; Mark is not placing on record the complete story of Christ's gospel in all its historical extension, but is announcing the "*beginning* of the Good News about Jesus Christ, the Son of God" (1:1). Jesus begins his ministry by proclaiming the Good News that the kingdom of God is at hand, a kingdom that will encompass all who are converted and who believe (1:15).

Mark's Gospel begins with a theophany, a vision seen only by Jesus. He sees the heavens torn apart, an allusion to Isaiah 64:1, part of a prayer that God may inaugurate the end-time *(eschaton)* as a new exodus. He sees the Spirit descending upon him (1:10), an allusion to Isaiah 63:11, 14, where God's Spirit is said to have come down upon the Israelites during the Exodus, just as in Exodus 19:11, 18, 20, God had come down upon Sinai to form God's people. The descent "like a dove" alludes to the dove as a symbol of Israel (e.g., Hos 11:11; Pss 68:13; 74:19). Jesus is thus designated as the representative of God's new people according to the Spirit. God endows Jesus with the Spirit and empowers him for the ministry that he is undertaking. The second aspect of the theophany is auditory: "Out of the heavens came a voice" (1:11). This allusion to Isaiah 42:1 attests that Jesus is the unique Son of God, the Servant of Yahweh, anointed with God's prophetic Spirit. In Isaiah 42:1, the servant in whom God delights is the one whom God has chosen for ministry. The words God speaks are also drawn from Psalm 2:7 in which God is described as solemnly addressing the words, "My son are you," to his anointed (Messiah) from the royal house of David.

The beginning of the Good News is God's word of love: "You are my Beloved" (1:11). The Good News is Jesus as the Beloved Son of God, the one in whom God delights, is the one in whom God's rule and kingdom are present and at work. Mark presumes that the Good News is still in the process of being communicated in the life of the community of those who bear the name of Christ. The kingdom comes when human minds and hearts discover that in Jesus they too have become the beloved of God. Through the gift of his Spirit they know the joy of God's love.

In common with the other New Testament writers, Mark is concerned to elicit an authentic response to the word of love spoken by God in Jesus. He interprets Christian responsiveness to the word in terms of the mystery of the Cross. The norm of Christian authenticity, the law of love, is the Way of the Cross traversed by God's Beloved Son. Mark's Gospel enjoys canonicity because the Church ("God's Beloved in Rome" and elsewhere; cf. Rom 1:7) believes that it truly expresses the meaning and demand of God's love for every age and for every culture. It presents us with the agenda for the coming of the kingdom in Jesus and for the community that follows him on his Way of the Cross.

Love affirms the concrete goodness of its objects. God's word of love, in Mark's narrative, is not an abstract concept but the affirmation of the concrete, particular, historically conditioned, and interpersonal goodness of the Beloved. In addressing Jesus as Beloved, God addresses all humankind. Jesus, in his concrete and particular humanity, is the word of love addressed by God to us. What is good about the Good News is its concreteness; the teacher and the healer from Nazareth is already doing what he will do at the end of time: uniting his human brothers and sisters with himself and with one another by drawing them into his filial relationship under the lordship of his Father's love.

Baptism, Transfiguration, the Cross: Signs of Acceptance

That Jesus is the Beloved and the Delight of the Father is the basic assumption of Mark's Gospel. Although explicit reference to the Father occurs only later in Mark's narrative (8:38; 11:25; 13:32; 14:36), it is clearly the Father who speaks at the baptism of Jesus. God's declaration, spoken as the heavens open and the Spirit descends, should control our reading and interpretation of all the complete and incomplete, successful and unsuccessful attempts to identify Jesus that follow throughout the gospel.

Historicist criticism reduces the understanding of the baptism to the question of whether it was an objective occurrence, a subjective vision of Jesus, an "experience," or an early Christian myth. Editorial analysis, in contrast, seizes on the theological importance the baptism had for Mark. For Mark, the marvelous reality of the Father's love for the Son, and the revelation of that reality, is the key to grasping the story of Jesus as Good News for all.

Mark presumes that his reader believes that what he relates is true. There is no provision for countering the skeptic who would object, "Jesus *says* that when he came out of the water . . ." To doubt the truth of the baptismal theophany is to range oneself with those who did not understand who Jesus was (cf. 2:7; 3:21-30; 6:2-3, etc.). At a deeper level, it is to range oneself with those who do not know the Father. We judge the truth of God by connaturality. Born again with Christ (cf. *connaître:* to know, to be *con-naître,* born with), we recognize the voice of Christ's Father because we recognize it as the Good News about Someone whom we already know—that we receive it as the expression of a reality we have already experienced.

In a parallel passage, Jesus is identified as the Beloved Son of the One who speaks from heaven at his Transfiguration and, in parabolic form, Jesus identifies himself as the Beloved Son who will be killed by the evil vintners (12:1-12). Who is Jesus, and from whence does he come? Heaven gives its answer in the baptism and Transfiguration. The only human being in Mark's Gospel to give the full answer is the centurion at Golgotha. The centurion is the only one to acknowledge Jesus as the "Son of God," to recognize the Beloved Son of him who speaks from heaven (15:39). The Father's recognition of the Beloved, Mark implies, is now finally shared by a human person, a representative of all the Gentiles who will follow him by making the same full confession of Christian faith.

Mark's narrative is structured around three authentic and full affirmations of Jesus' identity. In all three, Mark implies that only the Lover authentically and adequately recognizes and knows the Beloved. At the beginning (1:11) and during (9:7) the life story of Jesus, the Lover explicitly identifies him as the Beloved. Only through the death of Jesus for "the many" (10:45; 14:24) is the Gentile centurion, the archetype of the many, able to share the Lover's recognition of the Beloved.

In recounting Jesus' consistent repudiation of the apparently true confessions of demons and demoniacs, Mark implies that only the Lover can authentically and adequately confess the Beloved. The diabolically afflicted confess Jesus as "the Holy One of God" (1:24), the "Son of God" (3:11), and the "Son of God the Most High" (5:7). Mark might well be implying here that Christians who confess Jesus with their tongues but have no love for him in their hearts are really no different from the devils in their meaningless affirmations of Jesus as Lord. The only adequate invocation of the name of Jesus is as a prayer that he truly be Jesus, the One who saves. Only the one who is himself Beloved (and those to whom that Beloved chooses to reveal the Lover as their Lover—cf. Luke 10:22) can authentically and adequately acknowledge the saving love of God.

The same relationship of the Lover to the Beloved appears in traditions already known to Mark. The same word that Mark employs for beloved *(agapetos)* is used in the Pauline corpus with the same intention. No one, affirms Paul, is able to confess Jesus as Lord unless he or she has the Spirit (1 Cor 12:3), a Spirit who has poured out God's *agape* into our hearts (Rom 5:5), a gift that has made us God's *agapetoi,* God's beloved (Rom 1:7). Through the Beloved God purposed that we should be holy and blameless, predestining us in love, *en agape* (Eph 1:1-7).

Mark sums up the story of Jesus in these three affirmations of his divine Sonship; affirmations that make up the beginning, the middle, and the end of his life story. Jesus is fully awakened to his God-given meaning and value, mission and purpose from the beginning to the completion of his life story. Aware of the Love who has called him Beloved, Jesus is enabled to transmit to the "many," symbolized by the Gentile centurion, the transforming and saving reality of that love. Confessions that Jesus is the Son of God, which are purely notional and which do not proceed from the real apprehension and intense appetition of the love of God appropriated by the gift of the Spirit, are as worthless and meaningless as the confessions of the demons whom Jesus silences.

Baptism and Transfiguration

At the baptism the heavenly voice affirms Jesus as the Beloved Son. Why does Mark's narrative repeat this affirmation at the Transfiguration? Why does Mark recount the Transfiguration at all? Why does Mark not postpone his presentation of the glorious Son of God until after the resurrection?

Every life story requires an initiating vision. Just as Michelangelo "sees" the Pietà in the stone before he starts to sculpt, so the Jesus of Mark's Gospel sees the meaning of his life's story in the moment that he starts to tell it. Jesus' life and mission begin with the major statement of the vision from which all else springs. Mark presents Jesus' knowledge and vision of his own beloved Sonship as the energizing source and dynamic principle that binds the disparate elements of his life story together. We can in no way do that which we cannot, at least in some way, envision. The baptismal affirmation of Jesus as the Beloved Son of God gives Jesus the vision of who he is and what his life story should tell.

Mark structures his story so that the vision that initiates the life of Jesus is present throughout his entire life story. The appreciative and inspiring voice of the Father is heard by Jesus throughout the length of his saving mission. The baptismal affirmation of Jesus as Son can be likened to the flash of insight that, when understood and judged to be authentic, becomes the ever present principle of a continuous response. The baptismal voice defines Jesus as one who at core is uniquely in relation to the Father; it defines the character of the favor and authority he enjoys from heaven. The baptismal account seems to imply that it was Jesus alone who heard the voice; the voice testifies to the ontological basis of Jesus' ability to communicate the concrete goodness and joy of being loved by God. It is because Jesus is the unique Beloved and Delight of God that he can make us beloved and delightful. It is from this that all else flows.

At the Transfiguration, the heavenly voice comes almost as a response to Peter's exclamation. Peter and heaven are represented as speaking. At the Transfiguration the representatives of the new People of God share the vision and hear the voice. Jesus is represented as transforming; the Beloved is making us beloved. The Transfigured is transfiguring us. This impression is reinforced by Mark's portraying Jesus as being in dialogue with Moses and Elijah. Peter responds by wanting to hold the feast of tabernacles; to reenact the honeymoon period when God's people dwelt with God in the wilderness. God's affirmation of the Son as the Beloved is the basis for the foundation of a community, when God shall say to no-people, "You are my people" and shall call Unbeloved "my Beloved" (cf. Hos 2:23-24). At the baptism the heavenly voice declares, "You are my Son, the Beloved, in whom I delight." At the Transfiguration a command is added, "This is my Son, the Beloved; listen to him." In the narrative of the baptism the accent is on the Lover's delight in the Beloved; the accent in the Transfiguration narrative is on the Lover's authority that is invested in the Beloved. The Lover not only loves the Beloved but demands that others listen to the Beloved. At the Transfiguration the Father reveals the depth of authenticity of his love for Jesus; in loving his Beloved the Father–Lover reveals Godself as the Lover of all humankind. To be converted and to believe the Good News is to experience the concrete goodness of being loved through and in one's God-given acceptance of the Lover's Beloved.

If the baptismal narrative reveals Jesus as the person whose very existence is that of being loved and delighted in by God, the Transfiguration narrative reveals that love and delight/joy as constituting Jesus as the sacrament of God's love and delight/joy for all humankind. The transfigured humanity of Jesus is the outward and visible sign of the inward and invisible favor that infallibly brings about that which it declares. Mark would not be writing the story of the Beloved Christ if he and his hearers had not themselves already heard the voice that calls them "my Beloved." Mark is writing the story of the One who is the supreme Symbol (sacramental sign) of the Lover-Beloved relationship, the efficacious Symbol *(signum efficax)* that draws together *(symbolein)* all humankind to become that which they contemplate. Christ affects us as sacrament by communicating to us the faith, the inner eye of love, which enables us to apprehend our basic self-others-world-God relationship. Unlove, like the unclean spirits of Mark's Gospel apprehends that relationship in a radically different way. Unlove-made-loved (to create a new Hosean character) apprehends himself or herself as beloved in the Beloved. The same faith, the inner eye of love, that enables us to apprehend the Father's love for and delight in his Son, enables us to apprehend the Father's love for and delight in all humankind.

The Cross: Locus of Divine Love

The Cross is the consummation of the Transfiguration. The Transfiguration narrative is placed in the context of the predictions of the passion. The Transfiguration represents how the transcendent Son, the Beloved, who is apparently "only Jesus" (9:8) is effectively communicating his relationship with God through his Way of the Cross. The Beloved must suffer many things and be put to death (8:31; 9:31; 10:33) before he can become the source of love for all other human persons. By his life-giving death Jesus enables others to recognize him fully and authentically as the Beloved in whom they are beloved. No full confession of Christian faith is possible for Mark except as the fruit of Christ's death; otherwise, Jesus' passion and death would be implicitly interpreted as superfluous for the fulfillment of God's will. Jesus' rebuke to Peter for failing to grasp that the way is the Way of the Cross (8:33) is addressed by Mark to the readers of his gospel lest they forget the costly demands of God's love for those God calls to become the beloved. If love costs God what is most dear to God, so love will cost us what is most dear to us.

The Gentile centurion stands for the many for whom Christ's blood was poured out (14:24). "Truly," he declares, "was this man the Son of God" (15:39). Christ's death becomes the sacramental sign by which the many may know themselves to be the beloved in the Beloved. The centurion's confession of faith represents for Mark a full confession of faith in the divinity of the crucified and risen Son of God. It expresses the Easter faith of Mark's readers. There are no appearances of the risen Christ in the Markan narrative when it is shorn of its longer ending. The response of the women to the theophany is to say "nothing to a soul, for they were afraid" (16:8). The original Mark represents the women as being told to tell the disciples to go to Galilee (of the nations)—it is there they will find him. The affirmation of Jesus' Sonship is elicited in Mark not by an appearance of the risen Lord but by the outward appearance of the failure of a criminal's execution. There is an exquisite irony in the Jewish women being told to tell the disciples to look for him in Galilee of the Gentiles and their telling no one, when contrasted with the centurion of the Gentiles who confesses the Beloved Sonship of the Christ.

Jesus' instructions on discipleship implicitly articulate the word of God's love that is the giving up of his own life. His first instruction defines discipleship as suffering: we are to take up our Cross (8:34). His second instruction defines discipleship as service: we must be last of all and servant of all (9:35). His third instruction combines suffering with service: "Whoever would be great among you must be your servant, and whoever would be first among you must be slave of all. For the Son of Man came not to be served but to serve and to give his life as a ransom for many" (10:43-45). Jesus Christ is the Good News that we, by sharing his suffering and service, may become for ourselves and for others the beloved of God. In human terms the news of Christ's death is bad news; the goodness of the Good News is Jesus as the Beloved who can and does pour out his life.

Mark leaves no doubt about the fact that it was not possible during the historical ministry of Jesus to recognize his true Sonship from his miracles alone. Jesus was more than a miracle worker. Mark's account of Jesus' Way of the Cross is an implicit rebuke to those who think that God reveals Godself only in miracles. Even the wonder of the stone being rolled away is insufficient to elicit the obedience of the women. Fascination for miracle working implies a misguided esteem for self-sufficiency that would be an obstacle to recognizing the divine sufficiency of the Son who can lay down his life in failure. In response to the scribe's question, Jesus prays the *Sh'ma Yisroel,* the recognition of our obligation to love God and adds to it the obligation to love our neighbor (12:28-31). The three affirmations of Jesus' Sonship show Jesus as the living fulfillment of the divine demand to be loved. As the Beloved Son Jesus reveals what it is to love God as much as he reveals what it is to be loved by God. Mark's Good News is the news that the *Sh'ma Yisroel,* the *summa legis* of the Jew has been perfectly and completely fulfilled in the life-giving Cross of Jesus. Our justification lies not in the keeping of the Law but ultimately in the gift of God's Beloved.

Mark's narrative as a Way of the Cross is the implicit condemnation of all temptations to idolatry—to ever-to-be-frustrated attempts of humankind to control its own destiny by controlling and manipulating God. To contextualize the only fully authentic human confession of faith in the Cross of Jesus is the most radical condemnation of all our human refusals to let God be God and to let God's Beloved be *God's* Beloved. Mark structures his narrative to present Jesus as the One in whom all our inclinations to idolatry have been defeated. Jesus lives by God's approval and not by humankind's approval. The final words of Jesus on the Cross express his recognition of the supreme goodness of God. "My God, my God, why have you forsaken me?" (15:34). In the midst of pain, betrayal, and failure, Jesus, like the just man of the psalms, cries out to God. Jesus cries out his prayer at the ninth hour, when the trumpets called the people to the evening sacrifice and prayer at the Temple. Mark implies that Jesus is with the People of God for the fulfillment of their worship. The bystanders do not consider the words of Jesus' prayer as a cry of despair because they had to distort them to mock them, hearing "Eloi" and saying "Elijah" (15:36). If it had been a cry of despair they would have welcomed it as a vindication of their condemnation of Jesus for blasphemy. The bystanders deliberately misquote Jesus to make of his words not a psalm of trust but a cry of anguish. The death of God's Beloved is the supreme example of the just man who, though all things fail, even then gives praise to God. On the cross

Jesus abandons himself totally into the hands of God, an act of such total self-transcendence that, in Mark's narrative, it elicits the fullness of Christian faith: "Truly this man was the Son of God."

Excursus: Conflict Stories in Mark

The following conflict stories are those designated by such as Arland J. Hultgren in *Jesus and His Adversaries* (Minneapolis: Augsburg Publishing House, 1979) 26–27:

(1) There are eleven conflict stories in Mark, usually with parallels in Matthew and Luke:

2:1-12:	The Healing of the Paralytic (Matt 9:1-8; Luke 5:17-26).
2:15-17:	Eating with Tax Collectors and Sinners (Matt 9:10-13; Luke 5:29b-32).
2:18-22:	The Question About Fasting (Matt 9:14-15; Luke 5:33-35).
2:23-28:	Plucking Grain on the Sabbath (Matt 12:1-8; Luke 6:1-5).
3:1-5:	Healing on the Sabbath (Matt 12:9-13; Luke 6:6-10).
3:22-30:	The Beelzebul Controversy (Matt 12:22-32; Luke 11:14-23).
7:1-8:	The Tradition of the Elders (Matt 15:1-9).
10:2-9:	On Divorce (Matt 19:3-9).
11:27-33:	The Question About Authority (Matt 21:23-27; Luke 20:1-8).
12:13-17:	Paying Taxes to Caesar (Matt 22:15-22; Luke 20:20-26).
12:18-27:	On the Resurrection (Matt 22:23-33; Luke 20:27-40).

(2) There are two conflict stories in the special Lukan material:

13:10-17:	Healing the Crippled Woman on the Sabbath.
14:1-6:	Healing the Man with Dropsy on the Sabbath.

(3) *There are three conflict stories in Matthew based in part on Markan and Q materials:*

- 12:38-42: The Refusal of a Sign (in part from Mark 8:11-12 and Q; Luke 11:29-32).
- 22:34-40: The Double Commandment of Love (in part from Mark 12:38-42 and Q; Luke 10:25-28).
- 22:41-46: The Question About David's Son (in part from Mark 12:35-37).

(4) *There is one conflict story in Luke based in part on Markan material:*

- 7:36-50: The Sinful Woman at Simon's House (in part from Mark 14:3-9).

(5) *There is one conflict story in Q:*

Matt 12:22-32; Luke 11:14-23; The Beelzebul Controversy (see Mark 3:22-30).

Conflict stories, obviously, are but one way for the evangelists to express Jesus' struggle. The story of the demoniac in the Capernaum synagogue, for example, expresses the demons' sense that in Jesus they have met the victor in the cosmic conflict between good and evil: "You have come to destroy us, haven't you?" (Mark 1:24).

2

Matthew: God's Righteousness or Self-Righteousness?

God's Happiness

While the Greek gods rejoiced in their happiness without concerning themselves with that of humankind, the God of Israel is solicitous for the happiness of all, especially that of God's people. Happiness, in fact, is God's very self. Readers of the Bible discover in what true happiness consists and how they must seek it. Happy are they who fear God; they will be powerful and blessed (Ps 112:1-2). If one wishes to be assured of life, well-being, blessing, wealth (Prov 3:10), one must follow God's paths (Ps 1:1), walk in the Law (Ps 119:1), listen to wisdom (Prov 8:34-35), find it (Prov 3:13-14), practice oneself in it (Sir 14:20), look after the poor (Ps 41:2); in a word, be just. The Wisdom literature of the Bible guides its readers along the way of true happiness with God and others.

The devout and poor of Israel understand that with God they possess everything and that total self-surrender and limitless confidence is the way to happiness: "Happy are those who hope in him" (Isa 30:8); "Happy is the person who has confidence in you" (Ps 84:13). For the true Israelite, then, to fear God, to observe the Law and to listen to Wisdom is the way to happiness. It even means possessing it already; it means being with God for ever, experiencing "the fullness of joy in your presence" (Ps 6:11).

With the coming of Christ, all goods are virtually given and happiness finds in him both its ideal and fulfillment. Christ is the kingdom already present and he gives his faithful the supreme good that is the Holy Spirit, the pledge of the heavenly inheritance.

In Matthew's Gospel, Jesus, the herald of the kingdom, defines, proclaims, and promises true happiness to his disciples in the Beatitudes (5:3-12). In both their passive aspect (the poor, the mourning, the meek, the hungry, the persecuted) and their active aspect (the merciful, the single-hearted, the peacemakers), the Beatitudes mirror Jesus himself, the truly happy man, the embodiment of the joy that the kingdom brings. Jesus is what Jesus communicates: the joy/delight of God (Matt 3:17 = Mark 1:11 = Luke 3:22).

Jesus' Sermon on the Mount (Matt 5–7) defines his relation to the Law in terms of prophetic fulfillment and eschatological consummation. All prophecy, for Christians, reaches fulfillment in Jesus (5:18); consequently, the heart of religion for the Christian is not the Law of Moses but Jesus, its fulfillment. Matthew addresses himself to the question of the relation between the Law of Moses and Jesus Christ, Son of God and Son of Man. He answers the question in terms of the eschatological fulfillment of the Law and prophecy.

Just as the Law revealed God's way of happiness for Jews, Jesus, its fulfillment, reveals in his very person God's way of happiness by contrast in six antitheses (5:21-48). In six instances of Pentateuchal Law, Jesus contrasts what God said to the wilderness-generation of Israel at Sinai with what Jesus himself says to his disciples now. As is evident in the fourth antithesis (vv. 31–32), the basic contrast is between two acts of saying ("it was said . . . but *I* say"). The "it was said" is the reverent "divine passive," which has God as the understood agent.[1] That God is the understood speaker is confirmed by what immediately follows the "it was said": some law(s) of the Pentateuch, in either a word for word citation or a generalizing summary. In six instances of im-

---

[1] Examples of this usage are supplied by the passive verbs in the Beatitudes (shall be comforted, shall be satisfied, shall have mercy shown them, shall be called sons—each time with "by God" understood).

portant socioreligious institutions permitted or commanded by the written Mosaic Law, Jesus dares to contrast his word with God's word. In three cases (antitheses three, four, and five, on divorce, oaths and vows, and retaliation), Jesus revokes the letter of the Law and replaces it with his own diametrically opposed command. Despite the permissions and commands of the Law, there is to be no divorce, no oaths or vows, no legal retaliation. The claim that Jesus makes for the authority of his word astounds the crowds. At the end of his sermon (7:28-29), they are dumbstruck by his teaching authority. As regards the Law and authority over it, Jesus stands where God stands. Matthew makes this claim, not by using any title, but by emphasizing the authority and power *(exousia)* of Jesus' word.

Jesus as teacher turns to practical questions of piety. The Jewish practices of fasting (6:2-4), prayer (6:5-15), and almsgiving (6:16-18) are not rejected but rather corrected, in true prophet-like fashion, in the direction of a hidden, personal relationship with "your Father who sees in the secret place." Here the Son teaches his disciples how to live as true sons of this Father whom Jesus reveals. The trust, love, and God-centeredness of this filial relationship receives perfect expression in the Our Father (6:9-13).

Doing God's Will

Jesus summons his hearers to trust in the Father (6:25-34), to forbearance toward our brothers (7:1-5), to perseverance in prayer and in moral action (7:7-14). The disciples must strive to enter the narrow gate (7:13-14); they must match their claims with good deeds (7:15-20). For Jesus the eschatological judge will not be satisfied with the mere lip service of "Lord, lord," or with showy manifestations of special religious power, but only with the concrete doing of his Father's will. Jesus the Son of Man is the eschatological judge who judges us according to our deeds (e.g., 16:24-28; 24:37, 39; 24:42, 44; 25:31-46). The ultimate criterion of what *is* the will of the Father (7:21) is the authoritative word of Jesus (7:24, 26).[2] He teaches his words now with authority as the

---

[2] John P. Meier, *The Vision of Matthew* (New York: Paulist Press, 1978) 65.

Son of Man who will judge all humankind according to his authoritative words on the last day.

Matthew identifies the earthly Jesus, the risen Lord, and the judge at the last day with the Son of Man. Hence the importance of the final commission the risen Christ gives his disciples—"teaching them to observe all whatsoever I have commanded you" (28:19). The commandments that the earthly Jesus taught, that the disciples are now commissioned to teach by the risen Christ, will be the all-decisive norm when the Son of Man judges all humankind on the last day.

For Matthew the true disciple is not just one who has professed his or her faith in Jesus and been baptized; rather, it is one who does what Jesus has commanded; does *all* that Jesus has commanded in response to the will of God; and does all in the light of the great commandment of love of God above all and love of neighbor.

The tensional structure of Christian life throughout Matthew's Gospel is envisioned in terms of doing God's will as opposed to merely knowing and talking about it. His positive example is Jesus himself who does the will of his Father perfectly. His primary negative example is the caricatured "typical" Pharisee. His secondary negative example is the Christian of whom Jesus says: "You can tell a tree by its fruit. None of those who cry out, 'Lord, Lord,' will enter the kingdom of God but only the one who does the will of my Father in heaven" (7:20-21). It is this type of Christian who will say to Jesus after Jesus has condemned him: "Lord, when did we see you hungry or thirsty or away from home or naked, or ill or in prison and not attend to you in your needs?" (25:44). This type of Christian represents the tragedy of what might have been: the blindness of unlove to the grace and call of Love Itself.

The first words of Jesus in Matthew's Gospel characterize him as a doer of God's will.[3] When John tries to dissuade him from being baptized, Jesus insists, "we must do this if we would fulfill all of God's demands" (3:15). Throughout the entire gospel Jesus wholeheartedly responds to the demands of his Father's will/love.

---

[3] Peter F. Ellis, *Matthew: His Mind and His Message* (Collegeville: The Liturgical Press, 1974) 138–39.

This is especially true when Jesus voluntarily accepts the ordeal of the passion (26:42). He teaches his disciples to pray with the same spirit of total self-surrender to his heavenly Father: "Your will be done on earth as it is in heaven" (6:10). Seeking first the kingdom of God and God's righteousness (6:33) is the doing of God's will. It is a righteousness that must exceed that of the scribes and Pharisees (5:20); it may not be practiced in order to win human approval (6:1). Within the field of pulls and counterpulls at the heart of human consciousness, there is always the risk of self-deception in doing the right thing for the wrong motive, of self-glorification in opposition to the glory of God. Jesus is not in need of self-affirmation; his Father's affirming love/will suffices.

Through the call of Jesus, the Son of God, the disciples become the sons of God and brothers, those who are given a share in his company and so to live in the sphere of God's rule. Jesus imparts to his disciples his teaching about the will of God, so that it is binding on them and on the Christian community of faith for all time to come.

The disciples respond to the gracious call of Jesus with lives that reflect the greater righteousness (5:20). Matthew uses the term "righteousness" seven times (3:15; 5:6, 10, 20; 6:1, 33; 21:32). Although he alludes to the righteousness of the scribes and Pharisees (5:20), he speaks explicitly of the "righteousness of God" (cf. 6:33; also, 5:6) on the one hand and of the "righteousness of the disciples" (cf. 5:20; 6:1; also 5:10) on the other.

The righteousness of God is God's justice, which issues in salvation and judgment for humankind. Thus, for the disciples to "hunger and thirst for righteousness" (5:6) is for them to seek God and the establishment of God's rule over all humankind. Jesus promises that this longing will be satisfied. Similarly, the injunction to "seek first the kingdom of God and his righteousness" (6:33) is a summons to the disciples to live for the coming of the kingdom of God. Jesus exhorts his disciples to pray for the approaching rule of God (6:10)

Matthew associates the righteousness of the disciples with their doing the will of God, the heavenly Father (7:21; 12:50; 18:14; 21:31) or, to use a metaphor with their "producing fruit" (cf. 7:16-20; 12:33; 13:23; 21:43). For the disciples to be "persecuted on account of righteousness" (5:10) is for them to be persecuted for leading lives pleasing to God and consonant with their being in the sphere of his rule.

The Greater Righteousness: Be Perfect!

The righteousness that Jesus requires of his disciples (5:10) is not simply different in degree from that of the scribes and Pharisees but different in kind. Jesus requires a "greater righteousness" when he exhorts his disciples: "You, therefore, shall be perfect, as your heavenly Father is perfect" (5:48). They shall be wholehearted in their self-surrender and commitment to God.

Matthew employs the adjective "perfect" one other time in his story of the rich young man (19:21). The young man tells Jesus that he has observed all the commandments, and asks him whether there is anything that he lacks (19:16-20). Jesus replies, "If you would be perfect (whole, complete), go sell what you possess and give the money to the poor, and you will have treasure in heaven; and come, follow me" (19:21). Perfection (wholeness, completeness), the reward of which is eternal life, is associated with following Jesus. Discipleship is the proper context for observing the will of God, for doing the greater righteousness. The hallmark, the greater righteousness, of doing the will of God is the love of God above all and the love of neighbor (19:18-19; 22:37-39). The disciples must humble themselves before God, totally rely on God (18:3-4, 6, 10), and they will do the will of God as Jesus taught it (cf. 5:2–7:2). Toward the neighbor, the disciples manifest the rule of God's love as the servants of all and not as the lords of all (20:25, 26), as the least of all and not as the first of all (20:27).

Jesus himself is the greater righteousness which he proclaims and communicates. Matthew depicts Jesus as the Servant who proclaims righteousness/justice to the nations and will bring righteousness/justice to victory (12:18-21, citing Isa 42:1-4). Jesus criticizes the Pharisees for having neglected "the weightier matters of the law, justice and mercy and faith (23:23). The "gospel of the kingdom" (4:23; 9:35; 24:14; cf. 26:13) which Jesus proclaims and enacts is the way the world is made "right" or just before God.

The righteousness/justice which Jesus demands of his disciples is the moral activity which does God's will, the truly Christian morality which corresponds to the grace and demand of the Father, as revealed to the sons by the Son. True disciples are not merely to practice justice. Their righteousness/justice is to abound, to exceed, to overflow. Their morality is to show an exuberant richness and abundance proper to the new age of salvation, to the last days, to the "eschaton" Jesus has brought and taught.

The eschatological abundance of the greater righteousness has nothing to do with the Pharisees' scrupulous performance of the minutiae of the Law, all with a view to acquiring merit. The superabundance of Christian righteousness cannot lie in an intensified Pharisaism, but in a new eschatological quality to one's moral action.[4] This quality is manifest in a total obedience to God, a radical commitment to God and neighbor in both interior dispositions and exterior actions. Because Jesus gives his disciples the eschaton in his death and resurrection, he can demand eschatological morality from them. What is new about Christian morality/justice/righteousness, is ultimately Christ himself, the eschaton in person. The greater righteousness is the superabundance of Christian morality and its concomitant joy, the new quality of human life available in Christ.

Justice and Mercy

Matthew seems to confront two distinct groups that are causing difficulty in the community.[5] One consists of "enthusiasts" who seem to reject any legal constraint and take pride in their prophecy and mighty works (7:15-23). To these Matthew affirms the enduring validity of the law (5:17-20). At the same time, Matthew rejects a "Christian Pharisaism" which would turn the gospel into a rigid system of rights and duties, and argues that life in the Church is to be under the new law of mercy and love. Mercy is not

---

[4] John P. Meier, *The Vision of Matthew,* 237.

[5] John R. Donahue, S.J., *The Gospel in Parable* (Philadelphia: Fortress Press, 1988) 79. Donahue refers to Raymond E. Brown and John P. Meier, *Antioch and Rome* (New York: Paulist Press, 1983) 57–72.

an exception to the rule of justice. A person is perfect as the heavenly Father is perfect (5:48) when he or she relates to others with that mercy and love which he or she has received. In the parables of the Unmerciful Servant (18:23–35) and the Laborers in the Vineyard (20:1-16) Matthew's Jesus teaches his disciples that pursuit of justice/righteousness of the kingdom flows from the experience of unmerited forgiveness from God. They are to manifest it to others with the realization that God's justice is always joined with mercy and loving-kindness.[6] Inasmuch as God's will for us is always God's love for us, the justice that does God's will is always the justice that communicates God's love.

In the parable of the Unmerciful Servant (18:23-35), Matthew's Jesus summons us to repent or to have a change of heart (*metanoia*, 4:17). Jesus calls for a totally new way of viewing the world which shatters misunderstandings of the justice/righteousness of God. Behind the God who comes to expression in the parables of Jesus is the God of Hosea 2:19 in whom are joined righteousness, justice, steadfast love, and mercy.[7] Behind the image of the king stands the God of Jesus who summons us to be forgiving because we have experienced forgiveness. It cautions against a legalistic or closed way of experiencing life which filters the unexpected through the narrow categories of rights and duties. In the ministry of Jesus the parable could have applied to the religious leaders, who through the Law and the saving act of God in history have received mercy and forgiveness but would want to deny this to others.

In the parable of The Laborers in the Vineyard (20:1-16), Matthew's Jesus seems to upset the basic structure of an orderly society. Were the parable normative for economic life, chaos would result. Any interpretation of this parable must respect the fact that in this parable the order of justice is maintained. Even the complaining workers received what they had originally contracted, and to their complaint the owner responds, "I am not acting unjustly" (20:13). Justice forms the background against which

---

[6] John R. Donahue, S.J., *The Gospel in Parable*, 72.
[7] Ibid., 77.

goodness can appear as true goodness. The complaint of the disgruntled workers is, basically: "You have made them equal to us" (20:12). They are defining their personal worth in contrast to others; they are not so much angered by what happened to them as envious of the good fortune of the other workers. Their narrow understanding of justice/righteousness is the norm by which they judge others. They want to order the world by their norms which limit the master's freedom and exclude unexpected generosity. The final words of the owner, "Do you begrudge my generosity?" (20:15), underscores the tension between love and unlove within the human heart. Since in Matthew "the eye is the lamp of the body" (6:22) and "if your eye causes you to sin, pluck it out" (5:29), these servants allow their attitude to distort their whole way of viewing the world. What began as an act of goodness to them and unfolded as an act of generosity to others blinded them to the goodness of the owner and the good fortune of others.[8]

Jesus' parable, in the spirit of Old Testament prophecy, affirms that justice/righteousness must be wedded to love and mercy (Hos 2:19). Justice/righteousness cannot be used to separate those whom God would join together. Laws, in the tradition of Israel, are just when they create unity and harmony within the community.[9] Jesus proclaims a wholehearted love of neighbor, and even of the enemy, and speaks of a Father who makes the light (goodness) shine on the just and the unjust (5:43-46). This God loves the person who is faithful throughout the day as well as the one called at the last hour. This God's love is wholehearted towards all humankind; it is not communicated in degrees commensurate with human self-righteousness. In the light of such righteousness, Jesus was particularly concerned to address sinners rather than the righteous (9:13). True righteousness is always the free gift of God's wholehearted love for all. God loves all with all that God is; God does not love on a *quid pro quo* basis. There is no more or less in God totally self-giving and all-encompassing.

---

[8] Ibid., 83.

[9] Johannes Pederson, *Israel: Its Life and Culture* (London: Oxford University Press, 1926) 337–40.

Righteousness as Gift

The wider context for the parable of the Laborers in the Vineyard is Jesus' command to the disciples "to seek first God's kingdom and God's justice" (6:33). Though Matthew is in debt to his Jewish heritage for his understanding of justice, he redefines justice/righteousness in terms of God's generous and saving intervention on behalf of those whom others might see as outside the pale of God's loving care.[10] God's justice is different from human justice. It forgives unpayable debts and summons the disciples to live a life of forgiveness to others as an expression of gratitude. To do otherwise is to risk the ultimate/eschatological judgment pronounced on the unmerciful servant. God's justice/righteousness is not to be limited by human conceptions of a strict mathematical judgment where reward is in exact proportion to merit. Mercy and goodness do not compromise God's justice/righteousness. God's ways are not human ways. God's righteousness is not limited by human conceptions of justice that would preclude our experience of unmerited goodness.

Righteousness is essentially something given by God. It is therefore God who brings it about, which is true also of the kingdom in connection with which righteousness/justice is mentioned (6:33). Righteousness/justice also appears in the Beatitudes (6:33) as the inner substance and the fruit of salvation in God's kingdom. Here, too, it is clear that justice derives from the grace of God for the Beatitudes are a promise of the kingdom of God. The Good News of God's love and mercy is an invitation to a righteousness that is promised and given.

The scribes and the Pharisees could not see that righteousness is the gift of God, and so they did not submit to John's baptism (21:32). They murmured because God's calling of human persons was in the nature of a free gift (20:13-15).

Matthew reserves the predication "the righteous" for those of his contemporaries only whom the Son of Man will declare at the Last Judgment to have, in truth, done the will of God (13:43, 49;

---

[10] John R. Donahue, s.j., *The Gospel in Parable*, 34–85.

25:37, 46). Matthew's Jesus, who affirmed that his true relatives are those who do the will of his Father in heaven (7:21; 18:14), is Matthew's Son of Man, who will recognize them as his own at the Last Judgment.

Righteousness, for Matthew, characterizes the conduct of life that pleases God, that does God's will. To live righteously means to do God's will in all the areas of human existence. Righteousness, therefore, comprises all the virtues. Righteousness is the attitude of persons in conformity with the grace and call of God within all the contexts of their relational existence. It is the attitude of the children of God who share the Father's character as revealed in the Son (5:44-45). Its final manifestation is still to come: "Come, you whom my Father has blessed . . . and possess the kingdom prepared for you" (25:34).

The righteous are those whose conduct is approved by God (23:35). Those who "hunger and thirst for righteousness" live for God's approval (5:6; 6:33; 5:10, 20) rather than for human approval. God's approval is always a free gift.

Jesus lives for his Father's approval. Even though he appeared as an outcast (Isa 53:4; Matt 27:43-46), he was the Servant in whom the Father could finally be pleased (Isa 42:1; Matt 3:17). He knew right to the end how to "accomplish all justice" (Matt 3:15). He dies on the cross as God's obedient and trusting Son (27:33-44), and through his death enjoys his Father's approval for the forgiveness of sins (26:28). The wholehearted love of the Son in response to the wholehearted love of his Father inaugurates the kingdom of God's gracious rule (12:28; 16:21; 17:22).

The divine approval and the human rejection of the Father's crucified and risen Son reflects the tensional structure of human life, with its pulls and counterpulls, when confronted by the grace and call of God to do all that God requires. Within the human heart, the desire for human approval competes with the desire for God's approval. Jesus emphasizes above all the intention of the human heart as the essential and decisive element for enjoying God's gracious rule. Loving God above all is freedom for enjoying God above all in the kingdom prepared for us since the foundation of the world (25:34).

The Law of Love

For the Jesus of Matthew's Gospel the most radical law is the law of love, the essence of "the Law and the Prophets," and that which most distinguishes Jesus' teaching from that of the Pharisees.[11] The one who loves God above all and one's neighbor as oneself does all that God requires. In almost every place where Matthew treats the law of love, he does so in a context of polemic with the Pharisees and contrast between the Law of Moses and the law of Jesus. The messianic law of Jesus goes beyond the Law of Moses precisely in that it calls for loving all human persons, even enemies (5:43-48). The same emphasis on the more demanded of Christians for being "perfect" is the selling of all one owns to give it to the poor (19:16-22).

Matthew's Jesus concludes all the directions of his Sermon on the Mount with the love command: "So always treat others as you would like them to treat you" (7:12). Jesus thereby subordinates all the directions to the love commandment, the ground and goal of all the commandments. By saying, "That is the meaning of the Law and the Prophets" (7:12), Matthew implies that everything in the Law and the Prophets is not only summed up in the love command, but is subordinate and subject to the love command for its true interpretation.

Jesus' interpretation, as opposed to that of the Pharisees is shown to be grounded in the love commandment in the case of the disciples picking corn on the Sabbath (12:1-8) and the case of curing on the Sabbath (12:9-14). It is not said that the Sabbath law does not bind. What is said is that the law of love—feeding the hungry and curing the sick—supersedes the Sabbath law.

The love commandment, for Matthew's Jesus, is above all other commandments in importance, and all other commandments as a result must give way when there is conflict with the love commandment. What Jesus declares and what the Pharisees deny is the interpretation of the love commandment which Jesus had applied in the two test cases of 12:1-14. Where love of neighbor is in

---

[11] V. P. Furnish, *The Love Commandment in the New Testament* (Nashville: Abingdon, 1972) 74.

conflict with any other law, even the law of the Sabbath as in 12:1-14, the law of love takes precedence.

That this is Jesus' understanding of the law is borne out when Christians are told that Jesus' law demands that they be reconciled to one another before making an offering at the altar (5:23-24). Love of neighbor, manifested by forgiveness, is more important than the offering of sacrifice to God.

Matthew underscores the paramount importance of the love command in two other texts (9:13; 12:7) where he quotes Hosea: "What I want is mercy, not sacrifice" (Hos 6:6). He affirms that God's law of love take precedence over all other laws.

The clearest evidence for the supreme importance of the love commandment appears in the account of the Last Judgment (25:31-46). When all human persons stand before God in judgment to account for their observance of all that Jesus has commanded, they will be judged according to their observance or nonobservance of only one commandment—the law of love. Nothing whatever is said about any other commandment.

Pulls and Counterpulls within the Community

Through the gracious summons of Jesus, the Son of God, the disciples of Jesus become the sons of God and brothers, and enter into the sphere of God's kingly rule. In response to this gracious summons, the disciples reflect in their lives the greater righteousness that results from their doing the will of God as Jesus makes it known.

Matthew describes the community of faith in terms of the "kingdom." They are "sons of the kingdom" (3:9, 45; 13:38) to whom God has "given the kingdom" (5:9, 45; 13:38), who in Jesus, Son of God, share the forgiveness of the kingdom (1:21; 26:28; 27:38-54), who have been "instructed about the kingdom" (13:52), and hence know the "secrets of the kingdom" (13:11), who seek the "righteousness of the kingdom" (6:33) and have been entrusted with the "keys of the kingdom" (16:19), who pray fervently for the "coming of the kingdom" (6:10) and produce the "fruits of the kingdom" (13:8, 23; 21:43), and who at the consummation of the age will "enter the kingdom" (25:21, 23) and inherit it (5:3, 10; 25:34).

Although Matthew attributes to the members of the Christian community the status of being "the called" (22:14), he reserves the status of being "the elect" (22:14; 24:22, 24, 31) or "the righteous" (13:43, 49; 25:37, 46) for those members only to whom the Son of Man will grant it at the Final Judgment (25:46).

In the present age, Matthew's community of faith is caught up in the throes of the so-called messianic woes (24:8). Not only does it suffer persecution at the hands of the Jews (5:11-12; 10:17, 23; 13:21; 23:34) and tribulation at the hands of the Gentiles (13:21; 24:9), but it is also afflicted by internal difficulties. There are members who do not understand the message of the kingdom and consequently are without true faith (13:19), or who are false prophets and mislead other disciples (7:15-23; 24:11), or who abandon their faith because they cannot endure persecution or tribulation (13:21; 24:9-10). There are disciples whose faith remains sterile because they succumb to the cares of the world or to the seduction of wealth (13:22), or who deny Jesus, Son of God (10:33), or who despise others in the community (18:10), or betray fellow-disciples to Gentile opponents (24:10), or cause other disciples to lose their faith (18:6). There is also the threat of status-seeking in the community of faith (23:8-12), hatred among members (24:10), rampant lawlessness resulting in lovelessness (24:12), lukewarmness toward Christian duty (25:26), an unwillingness to forgive one's neighbor (18:35), and other evils that threaten the spiritual welfare of the community (15:19).

In response to this situation in which he at once affirms the presence of God's rule in his community but must catalogue its many aberrations from the will of God, Matthew directs the attention of his community of faith to the consummation of the age and the inauguration of the kingdom by Jesus, Son of Man (10:23; 13:30, 39-43, 49-50; 16:27-28; 19:28-29; 24:3, 27, 39, 42, 44; 25:31-46). Matthew does this in order that his community might view the present as decisively qualified by the future and recognize that the disciple must pursue life in the light of the approaching kingdom; for the God who will establish God's rule then is even now at work in the Son to motivate the disciple to do his will. Throughout this age, therefore, the life of the disciple and the community of faith in relation to the kingdom of heaven is characterized by this tension between present and future (e.g., 5:3-10, 19-20; 6:33; 7:21; 12:40; 13:40-41; 17:9; 24:27, 37, 38-39).

In the light of this eschatological tension at the heart of Christian life, Matthew boths warns and exhorts his community of faith. Negatively, he reminds them that the possession of wealth seriously threatens the disciple who would enter the future kingdom (19:23), that those who cause other disciples to lose their faith or who forfeit their own will be severely punished (18:6, 8-9), that the coming of Jesus, Son of Man, for judgment will take the unprepared by surprise (24:36-39, 40-42, 43-44, 50-51; 25:11-13, 24-30), that those who do not do the will of God in the present can be certain that their appeals to the Son of Man at the Final Judgment will avail them nothing (7:15-23), and that in this present age they dare never forget that the Christian community, too, will undergo judgment at the consummation (13:47-50; 24:45-51; 25:1-13, 14-30).

Positively, Matthew exhorts his community to envision their lives as being shaped by God's promises (5:3-10); to be diligent in offering their petitions to God (6:9-13); to practice piety that is pleasing to God with a view to the day when God will bestow upon them the eschatological reward (5:12; 6:4, 6, 18; 10:41-42); to emulate the Lord Jesus, Son of God, by following his Way of the Cross, thus finding one's life even while losing it (10:24-25, 33-39; 16:24-26); to have no fear of enemies but to commend themselves to the providential care of God (10:28-31) and to depend upon God as completely as does a child his or her father (18:3-4); to suffer persecution with joy as those who will inherit the kingdom (5:10-12); and to be like faithful servants (24:45; 25:21, 23) who are totally committed to doing the will of God (6:10, 33; 13:44, 45-46), being ever watchful and ready for the unexpected coming of Jesus, Son of Man (24:27, 32-35, 45-46; 25:10, 20-23).

Matthew views the Christian community of faith as a people whose existence is characterized by a tension between the present and future. Even now it lives in the sphere of God's gracious rule and has the commission to proclaim the gospel of the kingdom to all nations and to invite them to enter this sphere. Although the Christian community lives under God's rule, it is not immune to the forces of evil. It is exposed to the messianic woes and to afflictions from within and without. Matthew, nevertheless, assures his afflicted community that its risen and crucified Lord is with it always, even to the end of time (28:20). The last words of Jesus, who has been named Emmanuel (2:22-23), echo the name "God with us."

Matthew's church is to be a community in mission that will bear witness to the "gospel of the kingdom" in the awareness that they will face rejection and persecution.[12] The identity of the least of the brothers and sisters of Jesus (25:31-46) and their specific sufferings are to be interpreted from this perspective. The sufferings borne by the least of the brothers and sisters of Jesus are apostolic sufferings borne in proclaiming the gospel. The brothers and sisters of the Son of Man (25:31-46) are a church in mission which through its teaching and way of life gives witness to Jesus. In such preaching the disciple is not above the master (10:24). Just as Jesus suffered rejection and persecution, so too will his community. The community's witness is not simply to indict an evil world. It is to be a light so that all humankind will give glory to God (5:16).

The Call to Vigilance

Matthew concludes the public ministry of Jesus with a farewell speech of Jesus to his disciples. This final discourse functions as teaching and exhortation to the community as it lives between the resurrection and the return of Jesus. The discourse evokes an atmosphere of tension and expectation; likewise the time prior to the return is a challenge to responsibility, a time for decisions and actions that will influence the hearers' ultimate fate. Key phrases and motifs resonate throughout this section (24:32–25:46) which convey its distinctive flavor:[13]

"Watch therefore" (24:42; 25:13)
Unexpected returns or arrivals (24:37, 42-44, 50; 25:10, 19)
Delays in arrival (24:48; 25:5, 19)

---

[12] John R. Donahue, S.J., *The Gospel in Parable,* 122.
[13] John R. Donahue, S.J., *The Gospel in Parable,* 97–98.

The coming of the Son of Man (24:27, 30, 37, 44; 25:31)
Praises of faithful servants: "blessed" (24:46); "Well done, good and faithful servant" (25:21, 23); "blessed of my Father" (25:34)
The use of "Lord" (25:11, 24, 37, 44)
Exclusions from the presence of the returning Lord (24:51; 25:10, 30, 46)

The theme of the Final Judgment is prominent in Matthew's Gospel and no place more so than in these seven parousia parables. After the first three short parables which stress the need for watchfulness—the comparison with the days of Noah (24:37-39), the men in the field and the women at the mill (24:40-41), and the householder and the thief (24:42-44)—Matthew adds three longer parables (24:45–25:30) which complement this exhortation to vigilance with illustrations of responsible action. To watch means active and laborious service and not simply inactivity or passivity in the face of the imminent end.[14] These three parables along with the grand final scenario of judgment (25:31-46) provide insights into Christ's call to vigilance. Christian conversion is precarious. There is always the danger of hearts growing cold and of losing the opportunity for proper action. Vigilance is not merely waiting for the future but active commitment in the present which will determine the shape of our future. Presumption about a gracious future is as risky as misuse of the present. Inertia in the face of the eschaton is as reprehensible as reveling in its delay. The time before the end of history must be seen not only as gift but also as responsibility for and to our future under God.[15]

Matthew's story of the Last Judgment implies that Christians must be vigilant lest their hearts grow cold. It presents a juridical situation in which one group is called just (25:37, 46) because they have performed acts of mercy and loving-kindness to those in

---

[14] John R. Donahue, S.J., *The Gospel in Parable,* 98.

[15] John P. Meier, *Matthew* (Wilmington, Del.: Michael Glazier, 1980) 360, comments on the third servant in the Parable of the Talents: "Out of fear of failure, he has refused even to try to succeed."

need and therefore inherit the kingdom prepared from the foundation of the world; the other group is cursed because they neglected these deeds. Matthew's apocalyptic view of history affirms that the suffering and injustice which afflict this world will be bearable because the order of justice will be restored. The Son of Man will unmask sin and evil and reward goodness. The world will be made "right" again when acts of mercy and loving-kindness are shown to those most in need.[16] Jesus, who expresses the higher form of justice in concrete deeds of love, has inaugurated the end-time by his ministry, death, and resurrection. Christians must be vigilant that the benefits of the end-time already begun with Jesus—the true order of justice—be maintained in their acts of mercy and loving-kindness. The service which the Son of Man demands on behalf of others is a service which he has both proclaimed and embodied in the gift of his life for all others.

If doing the will of the Father is to love God with all that we are and our neighbor as ourselves (22:34-40), the Christian community must be vigilant not to miss the opportunities for welcoming the gift and answering the call of that love. Jesus' farewell speech implies the risk among his hearers of failed potential and missed opportunities for communion, community, and communications with God and neighbor in true love and friendship. It implies that God's vocation of humankind to such communion calls for free personal response; the human task demands the free exercise of responsibility. Yet, in their mysterious freedom, human beings can turn their back on God, their face from their neighbors. We idolize ourselves. When we return to God in response to the grace and call of Christ, we are opened to God's renewing love and reconciliation. Our deeds of mercy and loving-kindness to "the least of the brothers and sisters" (25:40, 45) of the Son of Man authenticate, even now, our communion in love and friendship with God and humankind. We are called not only to love the Son of Man in "the least of the brothers and sisters," but to be also the media through which the Son of Man himself loves them.

---

[16] John R. Donahue, s.j., *The Gospel in Parable,* 124.

3

Luke: Banquet Joy or Resentment?

God's Peace, Joy, and Salvation for All

Luke's story of Jesus is that of Israel's Messiah and God's Son in whom God inaugurates the time of salvation by fulfilling his promises to Israel and the nations and thus accomplishing his plan of salvation. The religious authorities of Luke's Gospel are Jesus' chief opponents.[1] Luke portrays the disciples as the followers of Jesus who are loyal yet spiritually immature.

Spatially, the world of Luke's Gospel story is made up of heaven, earth, and Hades. Although earth is open to both heaven and Hades (10:15), the boundaries separating these realms are nonetheless fixed. God has created earth as the dwelling place for humankind (cf. 10:21; 21:35). It is the theater of history. The history of Jesus' life, for example, is situated within the history of Israel (1:31-32), of the Roman Empire (2:1-2), of Palestine (3:1-2), and of the early Church (1:1-4).

Hades, in turn, is the underworld, where the souls of the wicked descend and remain until the Final Judgment. It is a place of extreme torment (16:22-24). Heaven, the opposite of Hades, is the abode of God (2:14; 19:38), his angels (1:19, 26; 2:15), the exalted Jesus (12:8; 22:69), and the righteous (6:23; 10:20; 12:8; 13:29; 18:22). In heaven, God dwells in glory, and because God's

---

[1] Jack Dean Kingsbury, *Conflict in Luke: Jesus, Authorities, Disciples* (Minneapolis: Fortress Press, 1991) xi.

rule encounters no opposition, peace reigns supreme (19:38). Peace, or salvation, is the gift that God, through Jesus Christ, would bestow on Israel and the Gentiles (2:14; Acts 10:34-36). Jesus of Nazareth, in whom God's rule is present, summons Israel to repentance and to discipleship, offering it peace and salvation (19:9-10, 42). After Jesus' ascension, the apostles proclaim repentance and salvation in his name. At a future time God has appointed, the crucified and risen Christ will return to inaugurate the restoration of all things and usher in God's rule in splendor (21:27, 29-31). At the same time, all humankind will witness the fulfillment of the prayer that Jesus has taught his disciples for the coming of God's kingdom (11:2).

God is the chief agent in Luke's Gospel story of Jesus. God guides the history of Israel, of Jesus, and of the Church. Signs of God's presence and guidance pervade Luke's entire story. Luke affirms God's guidance by speaking of God's purpose (7:30) or will (22:42), or of the things God determines (22:22). Luke's Jesus affirms his conviction that he discharges his ministry as the unique agent of God serving the purposes of God (4:18, 43; 9:48; 10:16; 13:34).

In Luke's Jesus, God is at work to accomplish God's plan of salvation. Jesus, therefore, is the measuring rod and supreme arbiter of what is good or bad, right or wrong, true or false. Those who align themselves with Jesus, the sign of God par excellence (11:3), "serve the purposes of God"(16:15). Those who refuse to align themselves with Jesus "reject the purposes of God" (7:30) and "serves the purposes of humans" (Acts 5:38-39). Therefore, whether one "serves the purposes of God or of humans" becomes the norm in Luke's narrative for evaluating the human spirit. In Jesus, God is in the midst of humankind proffering peace and salvation (2:30-32). To know Jesus, for Luke, is to know God: "All things have been delivered to me by my Father; and no one knows . . . who the Father is except the Son and any one to whom the Son chooses to reveal him" (10:22).

Luke's Jesus fulfills the messianic promises about the "Prince of Peace" (Isa 9:5) whose coming would inaugurate an age of peace for the entire creation (Isa 2:2-4; 11:1-9; 32:15-20). The songs of Zacharias (1:79), of the angels (2:14), and of Simeon

(2:29) in Luke's Gospel of the nativity herald God's gift of peace, happiness, and salvation in Jesus Christ. Jesus transforms and enriches humankind as the bearer of God's peace, happiness, and salvation. Just as the love that human persons have for each other is founded upon the love which God has for them in Jesus Christ, so the peace and happiness among human persons is founded upon the peace and happiness which God grants them in Jesus Christ.

Jesus neither brings nor promises his disciples peace as this world sees it (12:51). He gives the peace and happiness of God, a gift received in faith. It is available for those to whom Jesus Christ gives the command to go in peace (7:50; 8:48). Just as the prophets had denounced the false hopes held out by the words of peace spoken by false prophets (Jer 6:14; 8:11; Ezek 13:10; Mic 3:5), Jesus denounces the false notions of security and peace of his contemporaries (17:26-36; 19:42-44).

The peace and happiness of God's rule is the gift of God's messianic salvation (1:79; 2:14; 19:42) in Jesus Christ. It is a divinely wrought reality that transforms humankind, though it still awaits final fulfillment. It is a sign of God's new creation which has already begun, and it will be fully realized when the work of the new creation is complete.

Luke's Gospel underscores how the rule of God in Jesus Christ enriches humankind with the peace, joy, and happiness of the kingdom. The joyful assurance of belonging to God characterizes the disciples whose names are "written in heaven" (10:20). The disciples share the joy of Jesus in the Holy Spirit (10:21). Theirs is the joy of hearing and keeping the word of God in a community of faith where action flows from contemplation (10:38-41). Theirs is the joy of the servants whom the master finds waiting (12:37). The Father has given them a kingdom in which they may rejoice (12:32). Their participation in Christian life and worship prepares them for that joy (12:35; 17:26; 21:34).

Perhaps nowhere else in Luke-Acts has Luke given greater prominence to joy as in chapter 15 where the parables show that God (heaven) rejoices over one sinner who repents. Luke introduces this chapter with Jesus' association with tax collectors and sinners, and with the murmuring of the Pharisees and scribes who criticize Jesus for associating with sinners (15:1-2). The stress in this chapter is on the attitude of the elder son who, like the Pharisees and scribes, does not rejoice over the repentance of a sinner even though this is his brother just as the tax collectors and sinners should have been regarded as their brothers. They were all Jews and had the same God and Father. Therefore, the joy called for in these parables looks to Christ's saving of sinners, and summons us to rejoice over the repentance of a sinner as does our Father. The inability to rejoice in God's reconciling love for humankind manifests the absence of God's rule in human minds and hearts. The inability to enjoy God and God's goodness defines the spirit of Jesus' antagonists, the religious authorities. Luke shares the conviction of Paul that the kingdom of God consists in justice, peace, and joy in the Holy Spirit of Jesus Christ (Rom 14:17).

Joy, peace, blessing and praise characterize Jesus' going up to Jerusalem:

> As he was now drawing near, at the descent of the Mount of Olives, the whole multitude of the disciples began to *rejoice* and *praise* God with a loud voice for all the mighty works that they had seen saying, "*Blessed* is the King who comes in the name of the Lord! *Peace* in heaven and *glory* in the highest!" And some of the Pharisees in the multitude said to him, "Teacher, rebuke your disciples." He answered, "I tell you if these were silent, the very stones would cry out." And when he drew near and saw the city he wept over it, saying, "Would that even today you knew the things that make for *peace*! But now they are hid from your eyes. For the days shall come upon you, when your enemies . . . because you did not know the time of your visitation"(19:37-44).

The lament over Jerusalem implies what Luke means by peace.[2] Jerusalem does not recognize the salvific moment of Jesus' approach. The truth of her visitation is hidden from her eyes. Failure to realize who Jesus is and what he means for her is the failure to accept the peace of Jesus. It entails her consequent destruction at the hands of her enemies. The mighty works that God has done in

---

[2] Robert F. O'Toole, S.J., *The Unity of Luke's Theology* (Wilmington, Del.: Michael Glazier, 1984) 235–36.

Jesus merit joy, blessing, praise, and peace. Jesus laments because Jerusalem did not know the things that make for her peace.

The end of Luke's Gospel contains expressions of the joy, wonder, and blessing that Jesus communicates.[3] The question, "*Did not our hearts burn within* us while he talked to us on the road, while he opened to us the Scriptures?" (24:32) affirms the joy that the risen Lord communicates. Jesus appears among his disciples and says, "Peace to you. . . . And while they still disbelieved for *joy,* and *wondered,* he said, "Have you anything here to eat?" (24:36, 41).

The risen Christ fulfills God's eschatological promise of peace and happiness (Ps 85:8; Isa 26:12). The risen Christ communicates the joy of reconciliation and friendship with God. When Jesus interprets the Scriptures for his disciples, he relates his saving work to his gift of our peace with God: "Thus it is written, that the Christ should suffer and on the third day rise from the dead, and that repentance and forgiveness of sins should be preached in his name beginning at Jerusalem" (24:46-47). The "Peace" that the risen Christ communicates is a reality that comprehends salvation, joy, happiness, reconciliation, righteousness, friendship, wholeness, and blessing.[4]

With Jesus' word of peace went the actual bestowal of peace. Jesus communicates his peace to the woman who was a sinner with the words, "your faith has saved you; go in peace" (7:50). Jesus reconciles the woman to God in response to her faith in him. She knows the joy and peace of believing in Jesus. She has welcomed the peace of God in Jesus Christ. Jesus cures the woman with the flow of blood with the same word of peace: ". . . go in peace because your faith has saved you" (8:48). Because of their faith, both women benefit from the peace and wholeness that Jesus offers to all humankind.

---

[3] Ibid., 236.

[4] C. L. Mitton, "Peace in the NT," in George A. Buttrick, ed., *The Interpreter's Dictionary of the Bible,* vol. 3 (New York/Nashville: Abingdon Press, 1962) 706. Mitton underscores the comprehensive meaning of "peace" in the New Testament.

The Traits of Jesus

The traits that Jesus exhibits in Luke's Gospel correspond to the comprehensive meaning of the peace and wholeness that he communicates.[5]

In terms of his ministry, Jesus is authoritative in word and deed (4:32, 36; 5:24; 20:19). Empowered by the Spirit and impelled by God's plan of salvation, Jesus resists Satan, presents himself to Israel as God's Messiah, teaches, preaches, heals, exorcises demons, calls disciples, ministers to the socially disadvantaged, journeys to Jerusalem, clashes with his opponents who reject the benefit of God's peace, suffers and dies, is raised, appears to his disciples, and ascends to heaven. In all that Jesus is and does, God is reaching out to Israel and to all humankind with the gift of his peace, joy, and salvation.

Toward God, Jesus is the quintessential Servant and the Righteous One (2:43, 49; 10:22; 22:42; 23:47). Full of the Spirit and of one will with God, Jesus loves God more than self (4:3-4), worldly power and glory (4:5-9), or even his own life (23:46-47). Jesus' obedient self-surrender and self-abandonment to God achieves the salvation of humankind. The loving God of Jesus above all communicates the joy of God's peace to all.

Within himself, Jesus is the epitome of integrity and wholeness. There is no discrepancy between what he says and does. Jesus teaches his disciples to pray, forgive, renounce possessions, and take up their Cross, and he himself prays, forgives, surrenders his possessions, and endures the cross (11:1-14; 14:27-33; 23:33-34; also, 9:23).

Toward his disciples, Jesus is enabling, for he commissions them to ministry (5:1-11), summons them to come after him (5:27-29; 9:23; 14:27; 18:22), gathers them into community (6:13-16; 8:1-3), and empowers them for ministry first in Israel (9:1-6; 10:1-16) and then among all nations (24:44-49). Jesus is exemplary, for he holds himself up as the one the disciples are to emulate (6:40). He is faithful, for following his resurrection he renews table fellow-

---

[5] Jack Dean Kingsbury, *Conflict in Luke* (Minneapolis: Fortress Press, 1991). See chapter 2, "The Story of Jesus," 37–78.

ship with his disciples (24:28-31), guides the apostles and other disciples to spiritual maturity by enlightening them about God's plan of salvation in him (24:25-27, 44-47), and commissions the disciples, as his witnesses, to a ministry proclaiming repentance and forgiveness to all the nations (24:44-49).

Toward persons on the margins of society, Jesus is compassionate and outgoing. He blesses the poor, hungry, sorrowful, and excluded (6:20-23). He has table fellowship with sinners and others on the margins of society (5:29; 7:33-34, 36-50; 15:1). His gracing presence communicates the gift of God's peace and reconciliation. Jesus forgives, heals, or raises to life, respectively, the sinful woman (7:36-50), the woman with a hemorrhage (8:42-48), the stooped woman (13:10-17), and the widow's dead son (7:11-17). Jesus grants the Gentile centurion the request he makes through intermediaries that his slave be healed (7:2-10). He overrides the objections of the disciples and receives the infants brought to him for blessing (18:15-17). And Jesus opens paradise to the repentant thief who is crucified with him (23:40-43).

Toward the crowd, Jesus is compassionate and solicitous. He welcomes the people as they come to him (9:11), permits them to gather round him and follow him (5:15, 19; 7:9, 11; 8:4, 19; 9:11; 12:1; 14:25), teaches them (see 4:15; 5:3, 15; 6:17-18; 7:1; 9:11; 19:47-48; 21:37-38), tells them parables (see 8:4-8; 12:13-21), heals their sick and possessed (see 4:40-41; 5:15; 6:17-19; 7:21; 11:20; 13:32), feeds them (9:12-17), and above all summons them to become his disciples (see 9:23; 14:25-27). Jesus also confronts people with their need for repentance (see 11:29-32; 12:54; 13:3, 5). He chastises those who falsely attribute his authority to Satan (11:15) as sign-seeking (11:16), as hypocritical (12:54-56), and as those who will be overtaken by Jerusalem's destruction (21:23; 23:27-31).

Toward the religious authorities, Jesus is open, for he remains in conversation with them throughout his public ministry, accepts invitations from individual Pharisees to dine at their home (see 7:36; 11:37; 14:1), befriends certain elders on one occasion (7:3-6), and, on another, is warned by Pharisees about Herod Antipas' desire to kill him (13:31). Jesus is generally confrontational in dealing with the religious authorities. Jesus clashes with them for their failure to recognize that in him God is reaching out to summon Israel to repentance and salvation. Still, Jesus is forgiving towards the authorities. In the first of his three final utterances, Jesus calls on God to deliver his opponents from the guilt they have incurred in bringing him to the cross (23:34).

As regards his death, Jesus is one who obediently serves as God's supreme agent of salvation, peace, and reconciliation for all humankind. Jesus knows that through his death the new covenant People of God will be established who will bear witness of him to Israel and to all the nations (4:18-19; 9:22; 11:2, 13; 22:20, 27, 42; 24:44-49).

The Traits of the Disciples

The traits of the disciples in Luke's Gospel story imply the quality of their response to God's gift of peace and wholeness in Jesus Christ. Unlike Jesus who wholeheartedly "serves the purposes of God," the disciples exhibit conflicting traits. Although they do not fall away from Jesus, they nonetheless falter at times and "serve the purposes not of God, but of humans."

The disciples are attentive as the witnesses of Jesus' words and deeds. They are summoned to let their lives be shaped by what they see and hear of Jesus (see 24:48). They are called to mission (5:10), authoritative, and safeguarded, for Jesus empowers them, dispatches them on missions to Israel, and assures them of divine protection (see 9:1-6, 10; 10:1-16, 17-19; 22:35). The disciples are enlightened, for they are the recipients of divine revelation (10:21-24) and the mysteries of the kingdom (8:10). The disciples are obedient, for when Jesus commands, they comply (9:14-15, 21, 36; 19:28-35). The disciples are loyal and supportive, for they stand by Jesus on occasions of controversy. Their fidelity to Jesus makes them vulnerable, for they, too, incur the displeasure of his opponents (see 5:29-32, 33-35; 6:1-5).[6]

Despite their basic loyalty to Jesus, the disciples are prone to spiritual immaturity, for they do not understand the divine plan

---

[6] Jack Dean Kingsbury, *Conflict in Luke*. See chapter 4, "The Story of the Disciples," 109–39.

that God fulfills in Jesus' passion (9:44-45; 18:31-34). Caught in a storm on the lake, their faith falters and they become fearful (8:22-25). Unaware that a woman in the crowd has touched Jesus' garment, Peter becomes impertinent and chides Jesus for asking who touched him (8:42-48). Upon returning from a mission for which they had been endowed with power and authority (9:1-10), the disciples become perplexed by Jesus' challenge that they feed the crowd in the desert (9:12-13). Dulled by heavy sleep, Peter, James, and John experience only part of the revelation atop the mount of the Transfiguration and Peter "really did not know what he was saying" (9:32-33). When Jesus and the three descend from the mountain and join the nine disciples below, Jesus discovers that the nine, by not availing themselves of the power given them, were ineffectual at trying to heal a boy possessed by a demon (9:37-43). Twice, the disciples show themselves to be status-conscious in arguing over which of them would be greatest and in refusing children access to Jesus (9:46-48; 18:15-17). When John tells Jesus that the disciples tried to prevent a friendly exorcist from casting out demons in Jesus' name, Jesus reprimands the disciples for wanting to be exclusive in their dealing with the man (9:49-50). Jesus rebukes James and John for being vindictive when they ask his permission to call down fire from heaven to consume the Samaritans who refuse Jesus entry into their village (9:51-56). As the seventy-two rejoice over their power to subdue demons, Jesus cautions them that such joy is misplaced; for they ought rather to rejoice that their names are written in the book of life (10:17-20). In reminding Jesus that they have left all things to follow him, Peter in effect expresses the disciples' desire that Jesus assuage their anxiety about the future by telling them what is in store for them (18:28-30).

In an excess of self-confidence, Peter declares that he is ready to accompany Jesus to prison and even death (22:33). Peter is unable to believe Jesus' prediction of his denial (22:31-32). Peter denies being a follower of Jesus (22:54-62). The disciples watch Jesus' crucifixion in safety from a distance (23:49). When the women report that Jesus has been raised, the disciples dismiss their words as nonsense (24:1-11). When Jesus appears in their midst, they disbelieve for fear and think they see a ghost (24:36-43).

Only when the risen Christ enlightens them about the plan of salvation that God has accomplished in him do they finally attain to spiritual maturity (24:25-27, 44-46, 50-53).

The Traits of the Religious Authorities

The religious authorities of Luke's Gospel story are the antagonists of Jesus. The authorities "serve the purposes not of God, but of humans." Though they look upon themselves as righteous, they are in reality self-righteous. Their traits indicate that they are wrongly related to both God and humans. Their vision of themselves, others, the world, and God is distorted. They reject the baptism of John, repudiate Jesus, and despise the poor. In contrast to Jesus, who always "serves the purposes of God," the authorities are disposed to "serve the purposes of humans."

Most of their traits are forms of self-righteousness.[7] Because they refused to submit to John's baptism, the religious authorities "rejected the purpose of God for themselves" (7:30).[8] They affirmed in effect that they had no need of repentance and forgiveness (15:7). As they see themselves, they are already righteous (5:32; 18:9). Still, because John discharged his ministry on the authority of God, to reject John's baptism was to reject the gift and call of God to reconciliation and peace with God. Ironically, they believe that they stand in a right relationship with God, when in reality they stand in a wrong relationship with him. To be self-righteous is to stand in a wrong relationship with God (18:9-14); for self-approval cannot be equated with God's approval. Self-righteousness is always a form of self-idolatry and self-justification.

To stand in a wrong relationship with God always entails a form of idolatry, of substituting oneself or anything else for God. In Luke's story, to stand in a wrong relationship with God is to be a servant of Satan and incapable of perceiving reality from God's point of view. Luke's Satan shows Jesus all the kingdoms of the

---

[7] M. A. Powell, "The Religious Leaders in Luke: A Literary-Critical Study," in *Journal of Biblical Literature* 109 (1990) 95.

[8] Jack Dean Kingsbury, *Conflict in Luke*. See chapter 3, "The Story of the Authorities," 79–107.

world and offers them to him on the condition that Jesus worship him (4:5-7). The temptation episode underscores idolatry, substituting something for God, as the basic temptation. When Luke juxtaposes his remark that the Pharisees are "lovers of money" to Jesus's remark that one cannot serve God and mammon (16:13-14), he implies that they have succumbed to the temptation of idolatry, of self-sufficiency apart from God. They perceive reality from a purely human point of view (16:15).

In their relationship with God, the religious authorities have lost sight of what counts most. They busy themselves with seasoning herbs and neglect the love they should have for God (11:42). They are without true knowledge of God in the biblical sense of a knowledge that is rooted in love. They are, consequently, among those who fail to comprehend the secrets of God's kingdom (8:10). They possess a religious tradition about the right relationship with God that they have never personally appropriated for entering into that relationship (11:52). They do not understand to lead a life that pleases God. Their religious formalism is devoid of true love for God and humankind. It centers on self-righteousness, self-approval, and self-idolatry. They seek to appear righteous without being righteous. Jesus denounces them for their empty pretense as "fools" (11:39-40). The religious authorities are so devoid of true love and righteousness that they cannot grasp that, in Jesus, God is visiting Israel with the gift of his peace and reconciliation (19:42, 44; 23:34).

Luke calls attention to three religious authorities who have the traits that all true religious authorities should possess. These three serve as a foil or contrast for the others. Zechariah is a priest (1:5); Jarius is a leader of a synagogue (8:41); and Joseph of Arimathea is a member of the Sanhedrin but who opposed that body's resolve to have Jesus put to death (23:50-51). Whereas the authorities are self-righteous, Zechariah is "righteous and blameless" (1:6), Jarius is a man of great "faith" (8:41, 50), and Joseph is "good and righteous" (23:50). These three exemplary authorities in effect a reproach to the others.

Luke's story shows that self-righteousness is not only an unloving/wrong relationship with God, but also an unloving/wrong relationship with all others. Luke makes this point prior to Jesus' narration of the parable of the Pharisee and the publican: "He (Jesus) also told this parable to some who trusted in themselves that they were righteous and despised others" (18:9).

The religious authorities are self-important (16:15) and indifferent to any whom they do not regard as their equals (14:12-14). Because Simon the Pharisee does not recognize that he himself is in need of God's loving forgiveness, shows love neither toward the sinful woman nor even toward Jesus, his guest (7:36-50). The religious authorities regard with contempt all those living on the margins of society, such as sinners, toll-collectors, and the poor (see 5:29-32; 15:1-32; 16:19-31; 18:11). In their distorted view of righteousness, rigid adherence to the Law counted for more than love for others in need (6:1-5, 6-11). By the same token, they lay heavy burdens of regulations on the people without teaching them how to cope with these regulations (11:46).

The religious authorities value the external appearance of righteousness more than the inward reality of righteousness. Jesus rebukes them for their hypocrisy: "You are those who justify yourselves before humans, but God knows your hearts" (16:15; see also 12:1; 11:39, 44; 20:47). Jesus accuses the religious authorities of being inwardly full of violence and greed (11:39). Their religious posturing is a form of their self-importance. They lay claim to honor that, is not their due, exalting themselves over others (11:43; 20:46). Jesus deplores such false pretense, declaring categorically: "For what is exalted among humans is an abomination in the sight of God" (16:15).

The self-righteous religious authorities stand at odds with Jesus and his disciples. They show their antagonism toward Jesus in numerous ways. They accuse Jesus of speaking blasphemies against God when he forgives sins (5:21). They demand to know why the disciples violate custom and do not fast (5:33-39). They watch Jesus closely to see if he will heal on the Sabbath so as to bring charges against him (6:6-10). They are outraged when Jesus does heal and deliberate on what they might do to him (6:11). They impugn his integrity when he permits a woman known to be a sinner to touch him (7:39). They are surprised that Jesus does not wash before dinner (11:38). They sneer at him because of his teaching

(16:13-14). They object to both the people's view that Jesus is a prophet (7:16, 39) and the disciples' view that he is king (19:37-39).

Once Jesus begins his public ministry in Jerusalem, the religious authorities seek to destroy him (19:47). They engage him in controversy and challenge his authority to teach and to preach in the Temple (20:1-8). Following Jesus' narration of the parable of the vineyard, they are so angry that they want to seize him and hold back only for fear of the people (20:9-19). They send spies to entrap Jesus in a political misstatement about paying taxes to Caesar (20:20-25). They attempt to best him in controversy about rising from the dead (20:27-30).

The intensifying hatred of the religious authorities for Jesus finds expression in their desire to kill him (20:40; 22:2). They entice Judas to betrayal as the means by which to obtain custody of Jesus (22:3-6). They ally themselves with Satan to achieve their ends (22:53), and falsely charge Jesus before Pilate and Herod Antipas with being a revolutionary (23:2, 5, 10). They call for the release of the insurrectionist and murderer Barabbas and the crucifixion of the innocent Jesus (23:18-25). Their blind self-righteousness leads them to deny that Jesus is the Messiah, the Son of God (22:66-71), and to mock him as Messiah (22:63-65; 23:35).

Luke underscores the religious leaders' free and deliberate choosing of the death of Jesus.[9] They choose Barabbas and reject Jesus (23:18). Their shouting prevails, choosing Jesus to be crucified (23:23). Pilate gave sentence that their choice be granted (23:24). He released Barabbas whom they chose (23:25). And he handed Jesus over to their will (23:25). Culpable human behavior, Luke implies, entails free and deliberate choice.

Luke first narrows the agent of Jesus' betrayal from "the hands of men" (9:44) to "the Gentiles" (18:32) to "the scribes and chief priests" (20:20) to "Judas" who has been entered by "Satan" (22:4, 6, 48), and then he broadens the responsibility to implicate all of Israel, "the chief priests and the rulers and the people" (23:25). Jews, Gentiles, and Satan are all responsible for Jesus' death in

---

[9] J. Neyrey, *The Passion According to Luke* (New York: Paulist Press, 1985) 83.

accordance with the way determined by God (22:22).[10] God's gift of peace and reconciliation in Jesus Christ calls all humankind to decision within the pulls and counterpulls of a cosmic conflict that is the context for the universal story of all humankind. Jesus and the religious authorities represent the antipodes of the spiritual conflict within the heart and soul of every human being within that universal story.[11]

God in Daily Life

After a short preface, Luke's Gospel plunges us into God's intervention into ordinary human existence. Luke's infancy narratives (1:5–2:52) show different ways in which people's lives are touched by the Christ event (Elizabeth, Zechariah, Mary, Joseph, the shepherds, Simeon, Anna), and the angels announce that "today is born a savior" (2:11). Jesus begins his public ministry with a proclamation from Isaiah (61:1-2; 58:6) that he has come to proclaim Good News to the poor and release to the captives and that "today this Scripture has been fulfilled in your hearing" (4:16-22). The first chapters of Luke stress the presence of salvation in Jesus. Salvation begins with the coming of Christ and his life offers an example of the way to God.

Luke's frequent use of the word "today" or "daily" conveys the importance of the everyday lives of ordinary people which become the place where life is lost or gained. Those who witness Jesus' mighty works proclaim that they "have seen strange things today" (5:26). In a narrative paradigm of Christian conversion, Jesus announces that he will come to Zacchaeus's house "today," and after Zacchaeus announces his plans for almsgiving and restitution of injustice, Jesus says, "Today salvation has come to this house" (19:5, 9). Jesus responds to Herod that he casts out demons and cures "today and tomorrow" (13:32). Luke underscores the

---

[10] Arthur A. Just, Jr., *The Ongoing Feast: Table Fellowship and Eschatology at Emmaus* (Collegeville: The Liturgical Press, 1993) 127.

[11] John Navone and Thomas Cooper, *Tellers of the Word* (New York: LeJacq, 1981) 107–10.

immediacy with which salvation touches daily life by editing sayings from the tradition. Those who would follow Jesus must take up their Crosses "daily" (9:23; cf. Mark 8:34), and in Luke's version of the Lord's Prayer the petitioner asks, "Give us each day our daily bread" (11:3). Luke's Jesus invites his hearers to recognize the challenges and demands of God in their daily lives.

From the time of Christ's appearance something has been changed in human relationships (12:52). The "today" of Christ's presence (19:5, 9) is the fulfillment of messianic time and the beginning of eschatological time, even though the Second Coming is in some way more distant. The time of Christ and that of the Church are treated respectively in the Third Gospel and the Acts of the Apostles. Both constitute that eschatological time, inaugurated by Christ and extending throughout history. The life of Christ and that of the Church belong to the time of salvation.

The "today" of which Jesus speaks in his inaugural sermon (4:21) is the time within which a decision must be made for or against him. It is the time related to the historical past which it fulfills. It is the time related to the risen and exalted Christ who speaks and acts today. And it is the time related to all human persons who hear the word of God through Christ and his apostles. The time of salvation is "today," the continuing "today" that fulfills God's promises to his people and indicates the presence of God's rule/kingdom in Christ and his Church.

Summons to Conversion

The continuing "today" of salvation in Christ and his Church entails a summons to conversion. The mandate given to the disciples by the risen Jesus (24:44-49) picks up key themes of the gospel and reveals Luke's understanding of the postresurrectional mission of the Church. The disciples are to be witnesses of the cross and resurrection of Jesus, and repentance and the forgiveness of sins are to be preached in Christ's name to all the nations.

This commission recalls the angel's proclamation of the mission of John "to turn many of the children of Israel to the Lord their God" (1:16) and "to turn . . . the disobedient to the wisdom of the just" (1:17). Later Zechariah will prophesy that the visitation of the "Lord God of Israel" will bring about knowledge of salvation and the forgiveness of sin through the tender mercy of our God (1:77-78), and the public ministry of Jesus is prefaced by John's call for conversion (3:1-16).

Conversion, for Luke, involves a prior act where God offers forgiveness in Jesus. The response of faith involves a new way of living based on a new way of viewing the world. Luke's Jesus explains his mission as one of coming to call sinners to repentance (5:32). The religious authorities reject Jesus' call. Sinners have the humility and compunction to accept Jesus' call; they are willing to admit their sinfulness or the truth about themselves before God.

Salvation is at stake in the everyday unfolding of human life. It is a gift for the now or "today"; it can be won or lost in every now. Those who accept the gift of salvation enter into the joy of God. Luke's Jesus recounts three parables of mercy about the joy of God in the conversion and repentance of sinners (15:1-32). The parable of the Lost Sheep teaches that there is more joy in heaven over one sinner who does penance than for ninety-nine who have no need of it (15:7). The parable of the Lost Coin affirms the joy of heaven for even one sinner who repents (15:10); and the parable of the Prodigal Son expresses the same joy at the return of the lost son (15:13-24).

Luke's three parables of mercy imply the active role and initiative of God for the recovery of what God has lost. The parables of the Lost Sheep and Coin imply that conversion is the achievement of the divine search for what has been lost. The Father of the Lost Son awaits and welcomes his son who had been dead (15:10). Conversion, as these three parables of the lost and found make clear, is always an entry into the love and joy of God. In the subtle portrayal of redemptive love in these three parables, Jesus is the one in and through whom the joy and happiness of God are given to all humankind. Jesus himself is the efficacious sign of the peace and joy of God offered to humankind for new life (15:32). Repentance is viewed as our return to the person to whom we belong and who longs for our return. Conversion is not a condition but a consequence of God's love, a love that goes out to seek sinners before they repent.

Becoming Merciful/Compassionate

Thinking the things of God in Luke's story of Jesus is primarily a question of becoming merciful. Such thinking clashes with our instinctively human tendency to love friends and hate enemies, to give and to expect a return. Jesus calls us, in Luke's story, to be as merciful as our heavenly Father is merciful (6:36). He expresses the divine demand and enabling grace for a universal love without conditions or limits; for our heavenly Father is good even to the ungrateful and the wicked (6:35). Inasmuch as the literal translation of the imperative "be merciful" is "become merciful," Luke implies that the grace and call of God in Christ entail our lifelong struggle to overcome the self-serving and calculating tendencies that limit our freedom to merely *quid pro quo* relationships. Jesus invites his hearers to abandon such a petty existence and enter into the sphere of his heavenly Father's absolute and perfect freedom to love all others unconditionally. Jesus assures his hearers that life in this sphere is its own reward; for we shall become the sons and daughters of God (6:35). We need not be concerned about reciprocity from those who cannot or will not make a return because our reward for being merciful transcends every possible form of a merely human recompense. Just as children derive their life from their father, we derive our life from our heavenly Father whose life is one of universal love and mercy without limits or conditions. Because the Father is who he is, his true children will, as a matter of course, be like him in thoughts, words, and deeds of mercy/compassion.

Jesus' injunction to host the poor, the crippled, the lame, and the blind who cannot repay us (14:13) implies how God's ways transcend ours. Jesus promises that God will reward our deeds of compassion on the day that the good people rise from death (14:54). The eschatological note of Jesus' promise is reiterated in the dinner guest's exclamation: "How happy are those who will sit down at the feast in the kingdom of God!" (14:15). Selfless generosity is even now a sign of the kingdom's coming. In lives of selfless giving the just are even now rising to participate in the eschatological banquet in the kingdom of God. Theirs is even now the joy of the friends of God, deriving from God's life of universal love and outgoing compassion. They are even now sharing God's love and compassion that unite the messianic banquet community; and they are even now communicating the joy of their community and communion to others. Their joy, like all divine and human goodness, is outgoing; so, it is forever good to be with such joyful, divine, and human persons.

Luke's story of Jesus stresses how Jesus' table fellowship with sinners and others on the margin of society is both the manifestation and communication of divine mercy. These sinners receive the blessings of the divine mercy because they are poor, as Luke's first Beatitude announces, "Blessed are you poor, for yours is the kingdom of God" (6:20). The tax-collector, the Gentiles, and the sinners like Mary Magdalen, who could purchase a costly ointment for Jesus, were not economically poor. And yet they were poor in the sense that they recognized their poverty before God; they welcomed God's Messiah, God's salvation, and God's merciful forgiveness for their sins. And for all these benefits of God's mercy repayment was impossible.

Jesus' table fellowship with sinners and the poor characterized his whole mission of mercy, and was at the center of his controversy with the religious authorities. The poor in Luke's story of Jesus are all those whom the religious authorities considered, for one reason or another, as hopelessly excluded from the kingdom of God. They were the marginal persons living on the fringes of Jewish society precisely because they deviated from the religious ideals of the religious authorities. Both social and economic poverty fostered the receptivity requisite for welcoming the Messiah. The poor are persons who are not self-sufficient; consequently, they depend on the mercy/compassion of others. Self-righteousness is the trait of self-sufficient persons who have no felt-need for the merciful forgiveness of God in Jesus Christ. There is no place for the divine righteousness where human righteousness suffices.

Jesus' table fellowship with sinners and the poor also characterizes his mission of communicating the joy and happiness of God's merciful reconciliation and forgiveness. The significance of Jesus' table fellowship in Luke's story of Jesus (see 5:29-39; 7:33-50; 10:38-42; 11:37-52; 12:35-38; 13:29; 14:1-24; 15:1; 22:14-38;

24:20-49) derives from the prophetic and Wisdom literature of the Old Testament, which had developed the banquet theme as an expression of the perfect happiness which God has in store for his faithful at the end of time. The eschatological banquet symbolized the accomplishment of God's plan of salvation. It is doubtful that any of Jesus' Jewish hearers would have been unaware of the banquet theme and its significance. Jesus himself employed the wedding banquet as a symbol of ultimate happiness (12:35-38; 14:16-24).

Jesus' table fellowship/banquets were a realization of the messianic and eschatological prophecies; and at the same time they are only the beginning of the ultimate realization of these prophecies. They promise more; they are signs of the beginning of the eschatological banquet. Jesus' parable of the Prodigal Son explicitly links the joy of God's merciful forgiveness with the banquet theme and its messianic and eschatological connotations. The feast of celebration when the prodigal son returns home repentant (15:11-32) alludes to the joy of the eschatological feast. The vocabulary of the narrative is filled with the Lucan motif of joy: "rejoice/joy" (15:5, 7, 10, 32); "rejoice with" (15:6, 9); "make merry" (15:23, 32); and "music and dancing" (15:25). The climax of Luke's vocabulary of joy occurs where "to make merry" is linked to the divine imperative of feasting in the kingdom of God when a sinner repents (15:32). The joy of God's merciful heart going out to humankind is the joy of the reconciled.[12] The gift of God's merciful love and forgiveness creates the joyful communion, community, and communication of the eschatological banquet community.

Luke alone records the two statements from the cross, in which Jesus to the very end continues to express the mercy of God: "Father, forgive them; they do not know what they are doing" (23:34); "I promise you, this day you shall be with me in paradise" (23:43).

---

[12] Charles Homer Giblin, S.J., "Structural and Theological Considerations on Luke 15," in *The Catholic Biblical Quarterly* 24 (1962) 30–31. Giblin translates the father's response to his son's homecoming as "his heart went out to him." He notes the same occurs in other NT contexts rich with connotations of Christ's redemptive love: e.g., his heart goes out to the multitude who are like sheep without a shepherd (Mark 6:34; Matt 9:36).

The mercy of Jesus is the mercy of his Father, just as the life of Jesus is the life of his Father. Just as the Good Samaritan is identified as "the one who showed mercy" (10:37), it is Christ who shows his Father's mercy.

Excursus: Lukan Themes

Luke's themes have been studied comprehensively by John Navone, *Themes of St. Luke* (Rome: Gregorian University Press, 1970). Some of these themes are the following:

1. Luke's universalism: God's salvation is available to all persons and nations (2:31-32; 3:6; 4:24-30; 13:29-30; 14:15-24; 24:47), and which is given concrete expression in concern for sinners, Samaritans, Gentiles, and other outcasts of society.

2. The importance of women in the divine plan of salvation (Elizabeth, Mary, and Anna in chapters 1 and 2; see also 23:49, 55; 24:96-11) and as persons of great faith and responsibility before God (7:11-17, 36-50; 8:2-3; 10:38-42; 11:27-28; 13:10-17; 23:27-28, 49, 55; 24:6-11; see also the parables 15:8-10; 18:1-8).

3. The poor (1:48, 52; 3:11; 4:18; 6:20-21; 7:22; 12:33-34; 14:13, 21; 16:19-31; 18:22; 19:8).

4. Joy (1:14, 44; 2:10; 15:7, 10; 24:41, 52).

5. The Holy Spirit (prior to Jesus' birth, 1:35, 41, 67; 2:25-27; in Jesus' career, 4:1, 14, 18; 10:21; promised to witnesses, 24:49; see 11:13).

6. Prayer (5:16; 6:12; 9:18, 29-30; 11:1-13; 22:32, 39-46).

7. The banquet/meal theme. Jesus' table fellowship with sinners and others on the margin of society (5:29; 7:33-34, 36-50; 15:1) and meals as a setting for Jesus' teaching (5:31-39; 7:36-50; 10:38-42; 11:37-52; 14:1-24; 22:14-38; 24:20-49). The polyvalent symbol of "sitting at table" evokes both the eucharistic meal and the eschatological banquet (see 13:29; 22:29-30).

8. Divine necessity/"it is necessary" (2:49; 4:43; 9:22; 12:12; 13:14; 13:33; 17:25; 19:5; 22:37; 24:7, 26, 44).

9. Today (2:11; 3:22; 4:18, 21; 12:52; 19:5, 9; 23:43).

10. The dangers of wealth and its proper use (3:11-14; 6:24-25, 30; 12:15-34; 14:12-14; 16:1-13, 19-31; 18:22-25; 19:8).

"Parable of the Prodigal Son Invites Us to Rejoice over Repentant Sinners"[13]

The parable of the Prodigal Son (Luke 15:11-32) is an invitation to share in joy over the conversion of sinners. Christ invites his hearers to share in his joy of finding and saving what was lost. His attitude contrasts with that of the Pharisees who object to his welcoming publicans and sinners (Luke 15:1-2). The joy to be shared is principally Christ's joy manifested here and now as a reflection of heavenly joy. It is evident from the parable of the Prodigal son that not all who should share the joy of the father, who has found what was lost, actually do share it when the opportunity is offered to them. The parable ends on an upbeat note: the elder son is only gently rebuked; he has tactfully been offered an invitation in the father's explanation of his own joy, and we await his final reply. Will he accept?

The parable, an expression of God's mercy shown in Jesus' ministry, affirms the sort of love that must exist and be manifested between a father and his own son. Christ calls his hearers to conversion *(metanoia)*, a change of outlook and affection. Just as the elder son of the parable provided the father with an occasion to explain his joy, so the Pharisees provide Jesus with an occasion to explain God's plan of salvation which goes beyond strict justice because it is founded on intimate personal relationships. It is a love which is fully justified. The righteous must learn that love bestowed on the sinner is not an injustice to them; rather, it is something which they themselves must share if they are to understand the merciful ways of divine favor. This, in turn, implies a change of heart or conversion on their part.

---

[13] Authored by John Navone, S.J., and published in the *L'Osservatore Romano,* N. 39, 30 September 1991, p. 10.

Jesus bears witness in his dealings with tax collectors and sinners that God himself is at work and is gathering to himself his community. Jesus' activity is the way in which God's mercy is seen and realized. Jesus' divine forgiveness and divine joy is the theme of his own parables on that divine forgiveness and joy. The parable expresses the good news of the joy to be shared here and now. It is the joy of Jesus himself as he gathers in and welcomes sinners. It is he who comes to search and save what was lost (cf. Luke 19:1-10), and he implicitly invites the Pharisees to share with him the joy of his find. And it is Jesus to whom the character portrayal of the father most immediately applies; those who have "sinned against heaven and before thee" (15:18, 21) are those who are "drawing near" (15:1) to him. Those who seek an explanation, even though they are not entitled to one, are tactfully advised about their own need of a change of heart (conversion) and are invited to share in the joy that simply must be under these circumstances.

The circumstances which evoke this apparently disproportionate joy over what is found are, in turn, rooted in a set of personal relationships and dispositions. The intimate personal triad of father–son–brother is the heart of this parable, and perhaps the core of its theology. The literary fabric of the parable is such that this triple relationship is raised against the background of a servant-or-slave relationship to an owner. The younger son learned how good his father was when he looked for mercy from citizens of a country where he was a stranger, a serf, a veritable prisoner of his job. Evidently, his masters thought more of fattening their swine than of caring for their swineherds. And so the younger son's change of heart arose from the brutal facts which prompted self-pity. His change of heart was prompted by the thought that even the hired hands of his father's house received many times over what his own starvation diet provided. But the perfect expression of his contrition sprang from a memory of the sort of man his father was, and found utterance in his confession that he had sinned against heaven and before his father, and was unworthy to be called his son. The operative notion is his unworthiness to be called his father's son. The father's reaction is precisely that which his title signifies. He does not treat his son as an honored guest, but as a son. The ring he has put on his finger suggests a signet ring worn by the householder's son; the sandals distinguish the free man from the slave, and the best robe in the house completes the picture of one restored to the full status of sonship. The precise reason for the feast is stated in the emphatic phrase: "this son of mine" (15:22).

The elder son is introduced at the point of feasting and merrymaking. He has not been consulted or even warned in advance of this exceptional event. He seeks an explanation and is considerably irritated when informed of the reason: "Your brother has come back, and your father . . ." (15:27). His father reasons with him gently in words which must be supposed equivalent to an invitation to participate in the reunion feast. The elder son justifies himself, and in so doing discloses his real motivation. He is not merely envious. He simply fails to comprehend what it means to be a father or a son. His is the mentality of a servant or slave: "Look at all these years I have been working for you as a slave" (15:29). He regards the conduct of his father's business as a matter of precept, not of love: "I have never overstepped any command of yours"; and he seems to expect special treatment by way of payment ("at least a kid . . .") for the services rendered. Even his judgment on his brother's sin echoes his own sense of values and his lack of insight into the heart of his own father: "This son of yours devoured your livelihood . . ." (15:30). He sees his father as one who was deprived of property by a libertine son, a good-for-nothing who is depriving him (and perhaps the elder son) of even more. The father saw himself as one who lost and then regained a son—as much as if he had come back from the dead. The elder son's complaint thus reflects his judgment that the feast was meant to show what the younger son was worth (as the kid he felt he himself should have received would have been given in payment of what his long-standing services were worth). In fact, the feast was an expression of the father's heartfelt joy.

Since he cannot understand his father's love for the wayward son precisely as *his son,* he fails to grasp his own relationship to that other son; he even refuses to call that other son "brother." When he pointedly refers to his brother as "this son of yours" (15:30), his father replies by calling him with equal, but much more muted and tactful pointedness: "this brother of ours" (15:32). But the rebuke is administered with consummate mildness. For the elder son is affectionately called *teknon,* which is more affectionate than the regular Greek word for son *('uie).* He is told that all the father has is his. He is advised that he is simply not in a position to be paid as though he were a hired man; much less is he expected to work as a slave. He should have spontaneously joined in the rejoicing as one who understood how his own father's heart went out to the other son who was, after all, his own brother.

Jesus' rebuke to the mercenary-minded Pharisees (cf. Luke 16:14) could scarcely have been more mild or more appropriate to the situation as Luke has chosen to describe it: on the occasion of Jesus' eating and drinking with sinners, and his receiving them with joyful anticipation, the Pharisees voiced shocked surprise. Should they not share in Jesus' joy by changing their dispositions toward their brother and toward him whom they are to recognize as having a father's heart for all?

This is the parable of God's redemptive love for all. Jesus is the one in and through whom the heavenly joy is shown to humankind: the Father is thus seen in and through Jesus' contact or "mediation" with humankind. Jesus is the efficacious sign of the reconciliation and new life (15:32) offered to all. The divine-and-human love (presented as a totality, since it is seen as realized in the action of one-and-the-same Person) is also presented as the motive, for instance, of the younger son's act of perfect love and contrition (15:21).

Jesus tells this parable to transform our way of thinking, feeling and acting with regard to ourselves, others, and God. The parable is an invitation to share the mind and heart of Jesus himself, to participate in his way of being together with all others, divine and human. The Christian community of faith recounts the parable with the same transformational intent of its Lord whose gift of the Spirit enables us to grasp the meaning of the parable and embody it in our lives. The Spirit of Jesus reminds us of this parable and empowers us to embody its meaning and share it with others as the bearers of God's reconciling love, joy, and compassion. Jesus, the Parable of God, communicates his Spirit in his parables. God speaks in the parables of his Word Incarnate and inspires us to respond to them through the gift of his Spirit. The Word and Spirit of God transform all human life as the Ultimate Truth and Love which alone can satisfy the human mind and heart. Although we are ever restless for the fulfillment of all humankind at the consummation, we even now recognize something of that Ultimate Truth and Love in the parables and Spirit of Jesus Christ.

The Ungracious Refuser of Happiness/Salvation

The elder brother in Jesus' parable of the Prodigal Son corresponds to a stock character in biblical literature: the ungracious boor, the churlish lout, the surly and sullen refuser of festivities who is unresponsive and unwilling to participate in the joyful activities of the community. There is a tragic dimension to such characters, inasmuch as the festivities from which they exclude themselves are the salvation and eternal life that god offers. The biblical tradition associates the refusal of such festivities with misplaced priorities, with the implication that dire consequences follow upon the refusal of people to welcome God's happiness.

Refusers of Festivities in Jewish Scriptures

The Jewish Scriptures offer striking examples of the ungracious refuser of festivities. Jonah, for example, is banished to the belly of a fish while erstwhile pagan sailors experience a newfound fear of God (Jonah 1:16) and who at the end of the story pouts in anger because he disapproves of God's forgiveness extended to the city of Nineveh in its wholesale conversion, while Jonah had been hoping for an outpouring of divine judgment (Jonah 4:1-2). Pharaoh refuses repeated opportunities to allow the Israelites to hold a religious feast to the Lord, and Job's friends virtually miss the festivity represented by Job's restoration (Job 42:7-9). David's wife Michal is smitten with barrenness when she rebukes David for his dancing and celebrating with the ark of the covenant (2 Sam 6:14-23). At a national level, the same unreceptive and ungracious spirit is criticized by the prophets when Israel and Judah refuse to listen to/welcome God or return to God (Jer 13:10; Hos 11:5).

Refusers of Festivities in the New Testament

The Pharisees are the main refusers of festivities in the Gospels. They do not dance with the joyous nor lament with the mourners, and they accuse Jesus of gluttony, excessive drinking, and bad associations (Matt 11:16-19 and Luke 7:29-35). They refuse to rejoice with the man who has been healed of blindness (John 9). They are outraged that Jesus would receive sinners and eat with them (Luke 15:1-2). Throughout the Gospels the Pharisees not only refuse the offer of salvation themselves but also resentfully try to obstruct others from participating in the joy of salvation. The rich young ruler leaves Jesus sorrowfully after learning that he will have to relinquish his possessions to enter the kingdom, "for he had great possessions" (Matt 19:22). This is similar to King Agrippa, who refuses Paul's call to conversion: "In a short time you think to make me a Christian!" (Acts 26:28 RSV).

Society as such shows itself capable of the great refusal, as when Jesus weeps over Jerusalem, saying, "How often would I have gathered your children together as a hen gathers her brood under her wings, and you would not!" (Matt 23:27 RSV; see Jesus' statement in John 5:40 RSV that "you refuse to come to me that you may have life").

The ungracious refuser of festivities appears in Jesus' parables. The elder brother of the prodigal refuses to join the party given in honor of his younger brother's homecoming (Luke 15:25-32). Luke's Jesus recounts the parable of the wedding feast in which people preoccupied with worldly interests exclude themselves from the feast, symbolic of salvation and eternal happiness (14:16-24).

The Kingdom of God as a Universal Feast

The kingdom of God which Jesus proclaims is described in his parables as a great feast to which all people in every age are invited (Matt 8:11; 22:1-14; Luke 14:15-24). It is a joyful celebration of god's faithfulness to God's promises that extends from the first to the last moment of history. Moreover, the image of the kingdom of God as a great feast is portrayed as a marriage banquet, expressing the joy of the most intimate fellowship between the Son of God and his bride, believers from all ages of time (Matt 22:1-14; Rev 19:9). The marriage banquet symbolizes the graced time for celebrating the joyful communion of the Son of God and his people: "How can the guests of the bridegroom mourn while he is with them?" (Matt 9:15 NIV).

Jesus alludes to the eschatological banquet at the Last Supper when he says, "I will never again drink this fruit of the vine until the day that I drink it new with you in my Father's kingdom" (Matt 26:29 NRSV; Mark 14:25; Luke 22:18, 28-30).

The writer of Hebrews implies the consequences of refusing the grace and call of Jesus to his heavenly Father's banquet, when he asks, "How shall we escape if we refuse such a great salvation?" (Heb 3:3 RSV), adding, "See that you do not refuse him who is speaking" (Heb 12:25).[14]

---

[14] David B. Burrell, C.S.C., following the thought of Aquinas, treats the notion of sin as refusal in his book, *Creation in Three Traditions* (Notre Dame, Ind.: Notre Dame University Press, 1993). Refusal consists in the human capacity to withdraw oneself from the order of the divine intellect which predestines all humankind for the communion of friendship with God (*ST* I, q. 17, a. 1). Free agents can elicit absolute objective falsity by their capacity to work a paradoxical self-removal from that ordering which is the primary intent of the creator. Sin is the refusal to collaborate with the divine initiative for human fulfillment and happiness under the sovereignty of God's love.

Human beings are free to collaborate with divine grace or to hold back from entering into the dynamic of free action which is sin. Sin is not so much an action as it is a holding back from letting oneself be caught up into the full dynamic of God's saving action. What results from such a short circuit is nonaction rather than action.

In self-deception, for example, the tactic we employ is to put aside those deliberations which affect full-blooded action. By failing to spell out, either to ourselves or to others, our engagements, we allow ourselves to pursue an apparent good to the exclusion of the genuine good we would otherwise acknowledge. We may of course assign reasons to the failure, but these are excuses rather than reasons for acting. And if we think of reasons as causes for acting, then the action *as* an evil has no cause. Ontologically, it is attributable to a failure rather than to an intention, yet a failure for which we are responsible, since we are called upon as free agents to act intelligently rather than heedlessly. And what assures our being responsible for this failure in the case of self-deception, as the very expression implies, is our peripheral awareness of what it is that we are letting go. We can, as it were, sense ourselves failing to engage and so allowing our skewed dynamics of the situation to take over.

The agent who attempts to ape the creator and act in such a way as to be the total originator of its action does not so much act as fail to act. The radical capacity of free agents to refuse the intrinsic orientation of their natures assures that God is not the author of sin.

God has predestined all humankind for eternal happiness. That is what God wills to happen. Our eternal unhappiness is what God wills not to happen. Reprobation is what God permits to happen. The divine intention to grant all human beings a share in the very life of God is predestination (grace). Effectively withdrawing ourselves from the ordering of that divine intention is sin (pp. 120–27).

4

John: God's Glory or Self-Glorification?

Opposed Ways of Self-Understanding

There are two opposed ways of self-understanding in John's view of humankind, based on our rejection or acceptance of the Word of God. To the extent that we are centered on ourselves and our contingent world, we are blind to God's self-gift in Jesus Christ, the Word of God. Our self-confidence, based on the illusion of self-sufficiency, represents a radical turning away from God (see 15:5; 8:12; 11:10; 1 John 1:6). This is the sin of the world which separates us from God (see 8:51; 15:24); it is a rejection of the life, light, and spirit of God (see 9:39).

A diametrically opposed self-understanding characterizes persons who have radically accepted the gift of God in Jesus Christ. Their faith in Jesus Christ is a divine work (6:29), the gift of a new consciousness that derives from the Father's love for them, for no one can come to the Son unless the Father's love draws them (6:37-39; 10:28-29). Of ourselves, we have no knowledge of God, the Father of Jesus (15:22-24). A loving adherence to Jesus Christ in faith is the gift and work of God.

Love and Faith

In his account of Jesus' public ministry (John 1–12), John points out the all-important role love plays in the relations between the

Father and Son and between God and humankind.[1] In John's account of Jesus' last discourse (13–17) he sets about explaining this role. Finally, in his first letter, in which in four short chapters the Greek verb for love *(agapao)* and its derivatives (*agape* and *agapetos*) recur more frequently than in any other book of the New Testament, he completes his explanation by revealing the full depths of love's meaning.

Christian faith, for John, is "to believe in" Christ. By believing in Christ we become his disciples. Only by believing in Christ can we have the eternal life that goes to his disciples (6:29, 40). Peter declares faith the reason why the Twelve have become followers of Christ and explains their faith as faith in his identity as "the Holy One of God" (6:69). Christian faith means accepting Jesus for what he is as the Christ and Son of God sent or come into the world (11:27, 42-43; 17:18, 20-23).

The Son of God is God's own image. Entering human history in human form, he becomes the revelation of the transcendent God whom no one has at any time seen (1:18). To accept or reject God's revelation of Godself means to accept or reject God: "He who has seen me has seen the Father" (14:9). Christian faith means accepting Jesus as God's self-revelation to all humankind.

If Christian faith means fully accepting Christ for what he is, it cannot consist in mere intellectual recognition of his identity. Jesus reveals God's inner life to humankind by sharing it. Knowledge of God in the biblical/Semitic sense entails the intimate experience of sharing in God's life, or becoming God's child (17:3; 20:31). Christ's saving mission is that of communicating God's inner life/spirit to human persons as a reality they experience: "The Son of God has come and given us understanding that we may *know* the True One and *be in* the True One through the Son, Jesus Christ (1 John 5:20). Faith consists in our full acceptance of God's life in Jesus Christ: "To as many as accepted him he gave power to become children of God" (1:12). By faith we welcome

---

[1] Thomas Barrosse, C.S.C., "The Relationship of Love to Faith in St. John," in *Theological Studies* 18 (4) (December 1957) 538–45.

God's self-communication in Christ; it is God who makes us God's children.

Christ the light, God's saving self-manifestation, has come into the world. We must choose between accepting or rejecting him. The first twelve chapters of John's Gospel tell the story of the momentous choice made by Christ's contemporaries. The choice to accept or reject Christ divides humankind into two opposed camps.

Faith is the human response to the gift/offer of God's love; it is opposed by love of the darkness; it is accompanied by love of the light (3:14-21). God's sending the Son into the world on his saving mission is an act of love for the world (3:16). John affirms the universality of God's love for all humankind (3:16). If anyone fails to receive God's salvation in Christ, the responsibility does not lie with Christ. They condemn themselves by rejecting their only hope of salvation (3:18). The universality of Christ's mission expresses the universality of the divine love which inspires it.

Without human acceptance, God's love cannot be enjoyed. The offer of God's love calls for human receptivity. By corresponding, human beings allow God's love to bestow upon them eternal life (3:16) or salvation (3:17). By refusing, they reject the concrete expression and gift of God's love, Christ. Humankind must respond to God's love so that it can achieve its aims. This response if faith: "God so loved the world . . . that everyone who believes . . . may have eternal life (3:16). Faith, therefore, which means the acceptance of Christ, is acceptance of the concrete manifestation of God's saving love for us.

Love of the Darkness (Loves Opposed to Faith): John 3:16-21

Human beings fail to respond to God's love because of their love of the darkness: "The light has come into the world, yet human beings have loved the darkness rather than the light, because their deeds were evil. For everyone who does evil hates the light, lest his or her deed should be exposed. But everyone who does what is true comes to the light, that it may be clearly seen that his or her deeds have been performed in God" (13:16-21).

Christ declares himself the light of the world (8:12; 9:5; 12:46) to underscore his role in revealing and communicating God to humankind. Refusal to accept the light is refusal to accept or believe in Christ. Love of the darkness motivates this refusal.

Darkness means the absence of light; hence, in John it means absence of the light which is Christ. In fact, it is precisely the world without God—without the manifestation of God which is Christ—that is in the darkness. At Christ's coming "the light shines in the darkness" (1:5). We are free to leave the darkness and come to the light (12:35-36). If we refuse, we remain in the darkness: in the human state without Christ and therefore without God. To remain in the darkness is to remain by one's own choice in the state of humankind without God (12:46; cf. 1:5). To walk in the darkness means to live and act in accord with this state of separation from God (8:12; 12:35). It is a state of our own making that is associated with our evildoing. Our unwillingness to have our evildoing exposed means attachment to such behavior, refusal to give it up, or at least unwillingness to undergo the humiliation involved in having our evildoing exposed for what it is.

Darkness is the human condition resultant on our attachment to deeds done in opposition to God. It is an attachment to what we have or are apart from and without God. Because of our attachment to what we have independently of God, we refuse to accept the offer which a loving God makes to us of a share in God's life.

Love for Human Glory: John 12:43

The twelfth chapter of John's Gospel, the conclusion of his account of Christ's public ministry, clarifies the nature of the love opposed to faith. Many Jewish leaders, John notes, were convinced of the truth of Christ's claims; however, they refused to profess this conviction "that they might not be expelled from the synagogue" (12:42). Their fear of exclusion was based on their fear of losing human approval and respect: "For they loved the glory of human beings rather than the glory of God" (12:43).

Christ reproves our concern for human glory as an obstacle to faith after his having declared that he does not seek human glory (5:41). Jesus asks his hearers, "How can you believe in me, since you receive your glory from one another and do not seek the glory that comes from God alone?" (5:44). In another instance, the person who seeks human glory is described as one interested in self-promotion or self-glorification: "He who speaks of himself is seeking his own glory" (7:18). Seeking such glory implies abdicating all desire for the glory that comes from God alone. It is a quest for honor, admiration, praise, and approval given a person by other persons independently of God. Love for human glory is a love for an illusory greatness enjoyed apart from God. Like the love for the darkness, a state without God of our own making, it is a love for something we have independently of God. It is a love that prevents our acceptance of God's offer of Godself in Christ.

Love for One's Own Life: John 12:25

John's Jesus speaks of a love for self or love that would spare self which leads to losing eternal life: "He who loves his life loses it, and he who hates his life in this world will keep it for eternal life" (12:25). John's hating the life that one has in this world corresponds to one's sacrificing self for Christ's sake. Love of self is equated with seeking to save or spare self. Self-love, a love which values what we are and have in this world above Christ himself, leads to losing eternal life. The love that Christ condemns (12:25) is the inordinate love of self in preference to himself.

The immediate context does not set this self-love in opposition to faith. Evidently, however, if this love results in losing eternal life, it must be opposed to the faith by which we lay hold of eternal life.

John's Gospel, then, mentions three loves opposed to faith: love of the darkness (3:19), love of human glory (12:43), and love of self in this world (12:25). The first is one's love of one's unhappy state of separation from God: an attachment to the self and what the self has independently of God. The second is love for self-glorification that is independent of the glory that comes from God alone. The third is a love for what we are and have in this world in preference to Christ. All three are love of self independently of God. This is the love which results in hatred of Christ the light (3:20) and makes our faith-acceptance of Christ impossible.

Love of the World: 1 John 2:15-16

In his first letter, John speaks of a love that excludes union with God and, therefore, the faith that makes such union possible:

> Do not love the world or the things in the world. If anyone loves the world, love for the Father is not in him. For all that is in the world, the lust of the flesh and the lust of the eyes and the pride of life, is not of the Father, but of the world (1 John 2:15-16).

The "world," for John is the personification of the human forces which oppose the realization of God's saving designs (1 John 3:13; 4:4-5, 19). God's adversary, the devil, holds sway over the world (1 John 3:8, 10; 4:4-5; 5:18-19). Only faith in Christ, which unites us with God, can conquer the world and "one who is in the world" (1 John 5:4-5). Love of the world means love of the forces that oppose God's self-gift to humankind. Love for the world is by its nature opposed to God and, therefore, cannot be of or from the Father. John shows this irreconcilability in listing what the world contains: the lust of the flesh, the lust of the eyes, and the pride of life. The first two are craving for self-satisfaction; the third is self-idolatry. These three forms of self-love seek self-fulfillment independently of God or without regard for God. These culpable forms of love preclude faith and communion with God. They imply a godless state of unbridled self-seeking that leads to hatred of Christ the light.

Love for the Glory of God (Loves Associated with Faith): John 12:43

When explaining why many of the Jewish leaders, though convinced of Christ's mission, refused to believe in him, John affirms, "They loved human glory rather than the glory of God" (12:43). John implies that had they loved the glory of God, they would not have hesitated to believe in Christ. Love for the glory of God is linked to faith and opposed to love for the glory of humanity.

Since love for human approval is given by human beings, love for the glory of God is love for the approval given by God. In situations where Christ criticizes the desire for human glory, he commends seeking the glory or approval that comes from God (5:41, 44; 8:50, 54).

Divine glory is the divine excellence proper to God. The Son of God made man has it but, like everything else which he has, he has it from the Father. The Son's glory is the glory which the Father has and which the Father has given to him as Son (1:14; 17:5). Christ "manifests his glory" by manifesting his proper excellence, by showing himself for what he really is as the Son of God made man (1:14; 2:11; 11:4). His saving mission is that of leading humankind to recognize him for what he is through faith in him. By carrying out his mission, he reveals both his identity and excellence. In other words, he manifests his glory as the only-begotten Son of the Father (1:14).

The manifestation of the Son's glory is the manifestation of the Father's glory: "He who has seen me has seen the Father" (14:9). The Son become man is the manifestation of the Father's divinity, since his divinity is also the Father's. The Father, therefore, is necessarily glorified with the Son because the manifestation of the excellence of either one is of itself a manifestation of the excellence or glory of the other.[2]

The Father glorifies the Son in that he communicates his own excellence or glory to the Son and, sending him into the world, manifests it in him. But by that very manifestation of the Son's

---

[2] Thomas Barrosse, C.S.C., "The Relationship of Love to Faith in St. John," in *Theological Studies* 18 (4) (December 1957) 553.

glory he also manifests his own glory or glorifies himself (11:4, 40; 12:23, 28; 13:31-32; 17:1). The Son glorifies the Father by manifesting the Father's identity or excellence. In doing so, he necessarily manifests his own glory at the same time (17:1; also, 1:14; 7:18; 8:50, 54), for this is the very same "name" or excellence that the Father has given him (17:7, 11-12). This is especially true of both the passion and resurrection, which appear as both Christ's own glorification by the Father (7:39; 12:16, 23; 13:31-32; 17:1-2) and as Christ's principal means of glorifying the Father (13:31-32; 17:1-2). By the very same act the Son is honored and glorified by the Father and honors and glorifies the Father, because what is manifested is equally possessed by both.

What is true of the relations of the Son and the Father is true also of the relations of the disciples and Christ. If the Father has given glory to him, Christ has given that same glory to them (17:22). Through Christ they share in God's life, divinity, excellence, or glory. They therefore have glory from God which is a share in God's own glory. By living as Christians should, the disciples manifest the divine reality/excellence which they have from him. This outward manifestation in their daily lives of the divine life within them glorifies Christ (17:10) and the Father (15:8) or, in other words, manifests the divine glory or excellence in which they share (17:22). Their lives glorify God because they are manifestations of divine life or glory.

God honors the disciples by uniting them with Christ, by letting them "see" or share in Christ's excellence/glory (see 17:24).[3] Christian life is a share in the divine life or excellence. The disciples have this life from God who does not give it to them once and for all at their initial acceptance of Christ but continually communicates it to them.[4] God's giving them a participation in

---

[3] See John 3:36 where "seeing" life is equivalent to having it.

[4] See John 14:23 on the abiding presence of the Father and the Son in the disciples: 6:57-58 on the abiding and vivifying presence of the Son; 7:37-39; 14:16, 26; 15:26; 16:13 on the Spirit's active presence in the disciples; according to 17:11, the Father must "keep" the disciples in his name or in communion with himself.

this own life/excellence/glory is God's "glorification" of them. Consequently, whenever they do anything that manifests their union with Christ, the disciples not only honor/glorify God by manifesting God's excellence and glory in their action; they *are glorified* by God who is giving them an active participation in God's own life and excellence/glory.

Christian love for the glory of God refers both to the will to glorify God and the will to have glory/approval from God. God is glorified by God's very self-giving by which God glorifies us: by our sharing and manifesting God's own life or glory, given to us. Love for the glory of God is our disposition and will to have a borrowed glory that comes from God and whose possession glorifies/evidences God. This is the only kind of excellence possible for a creature, which by its very definition is totally dependent on God for all that it is and has. Love for the glory of God is opposed to the disordered self-love/self-idolatry by which persons seek honor for themselves independently of God. Such desire for an independent excellence excludes of itself all readiness to accept a borrowed excellence/glory from God. Readiness to welcome a participation in God's glory/excellence, on the other hand, inspires and makes possible the faith which accepts Jesus Christ for what he is as the Son of God come to give all a share in God's life and glory.[5]

Love for the Light: John 3:19

If persons who refuse to draw near to the light because they have loved the darkness rather than the light (3:19), then those who accept the light have the contrary disposition of loving the light rather than the darkness. Persons who come to the light by faith love the light and "do what is true," manifesting deeds "done in

---

[5] Certain Johannine texts (see 2:11, as also 1:14 compared with 1:7-13) make faith our response to the manifestation of Christ's glory. This is another way of affirming the idea of John 1–12: the Son is God's manifestation and offer of himself to us. By faith we accept him for what he shows himself to be and is.

God" (3:21). Their deeds are in accord with God's will and, therefore, express God's love. Their deeds are done under God's inspiration and guidance. Such persons have something of God within them (God's Holy Spirit, inspirations and acts fulfilling God's will). They are responsive to God and therefore prepared to accept God's offer of Godself in Christ.

Faith is that coming to the light by fully accepting the gift of Godself in Christ. By accepting God we give up our independent life to become a child of God and participate in God's life. The love of the light is the readiness to have a borrowed glory, a God-given excellence; it is a love for the glory/excellence/life of God.

Love for Christ: John 8:42-47

John's Christ proclaims a love which only those have who come by faith to Christ the light:

> If God were your Father, you would love me, for I proceeded and came forth from God; I came not of my own accord, but he sent me. Why do you not understand what I say? It is because you cannot bear to hear my word. You are of your father the devil, and your will is to do your father's desires. He was a murderer from the beginning, and has nothing to do with the truth, because there is no truth in him. When he lies, he speaks according to his nature, for he is a liar and the father of lies. But because I tell the truth, you do not believe me. Which of you can convict me of sin? If I tell the truth, why do you not believe me? He who is of God hears the words of God. The reason why you do not hear is that you are not of God (8:42-47).

Persons who have God as a father have something of God within them. They love Christ and welcome God's words as they are spoken by Christ. There is a connection between love for Christ and readiness to put oneself at God's disposal. Persons who are of God love Christ because Christ is of God (8:42). Persons who are of God have God as a father and accept Christ by faith as coming from God. They recognize Christ as God's manifestation and offer of Godself/life to all humankind. Accepting Christ is accepting God; loving Christ is loving the glory/excellence of God.

Love of God:
John 5:40-44 and 1 John 2:15

Christ declares the Jews' rejection of himself proves that they do not have the "love of God" within them (5:42). If they had the "love of God" within them, they would accept him and show interest in the glory of God (5:44). The "love of God" means God's own love (with which God loves). That love grounds love from God (come from or given by God), or love for God. There is no love for God that is independent of God's own love as its source. Love for the glory of God and the light and Christ is a participation in God's own love.

The "love of God" reappears in 1 John 2:15: "If anyone loves the world, the love of the Father is not in him." To love the world in John's sense of a culpable love is always a form of idolatry, a substitution of the creature for the creator as our supreme good. Such love is based on untruth, illusion, and self-deception. As such, it bears witness to "the father of lies" (John 8:44).

Cosmic Conflict

There is a cosmic conflict in John's writings between Jesus and the "prince of this world" (John 12:31; 16:11). In the cosmic dialectic between good and evil, experienced in all human life, John underscores the role of Satan (13:2, 27; 14:30) only to proclaim his final defeat. At the very moment when he believes himself certain of victory, the "prince of this world" is "cast down" (12:31). The love and obedience of the Son triumph over the forces of evil that would deface/deform the beauty of God's true image and likeness in humankind.[6]

---

[6] John Navone, *Enjoying God's Beauty* (Collegeville: The Liturgical Press, 1999) 92–93.

John applies to Jesus, the protagonist of the cosmic conflict between good and evil, the word "glory." It expresses Jesus' very nature, the hidden aspect of being which is revealed to faith alone. John applies to a man a word which formerly described the manifestation in power of Godself. It had never been applied to prophet, king, priest, or man in the Bible. Never before had a sentence even remotely resembling the following been written about a man: "He manifested his glory and his disciples believed in him" (2:11). Only one thing could be meant by applying it to Jesus: God had appeared on earth and had been revealed in all God's power in Jesus. John underscores the essential sameness of the glory of God and the glory of Jesus, for example, "in him (the Son of Man) God is glorified"; "if you believe you will see the glory of God" (13:31; 11:40). These two "glories" are one. John remarks in the prologue to his gospel that it is the interrelation of Father and Son—Jesus' glory was "glory as of the only Son from the Father, full of grace and truth" (1:14). By the use of the word "glory" John understands his gospel as the narrative of a divine appearance, where fire, thunder, and lightning have given place to the appearance of a son of man, Jesus, who called God his Father.

The glory of Jesus manifests the nature, character, and power of God under the conditions of life in time and space. It is the transforming beauty of God's supreme goodness and self-giving love in Jesus Christ that is recognized only by those who have faith. Jesus brings the transforming radiance of God within human experience and expresses it most perfectly in his loving self-gift on the cross for our salvation. John describes the passion as "the hour" of the "exaltation" and "glorification" of the Son of Man (12:33-34). This exaltation/glorification saves the world. Jesus wanted his friends to share in that glory that he possessed from the Father before the creation of the world (17:5), and from that moment he communicated to them "the glory you have given me, I have given to them that they may be one as we are one" (17:22). The principle of unity among the redeemed is the glory of Christ radiant among them. Jesus manifests the transfiguring power of his supreme goodness and self-giving love among them; he is "glorified in them."

Beginning with Jesus and by means of Jesus who is the "true light" (1:9), but also by means of Christians who have welcomed his light and life and put it into practice through their love for others, God's kingdom of light spreads outwards and forces the darkness to yield. Wherever the Father's self-giving love in Jesus enlightens and transforms human persons, the darkness of unlove is passing away (1 John 2:8). Through the transforming light of Jesus we become the children of light through a creative act of God that recalls the original creation of light. Paul expressed this parallel: "For it is God who said, 'Let light shine out of darkness,' who has shone in our hearts to give the light of the knowledge of the glory of God in the face of Christ" (2 Cor 4:6; cf. Gen 1:3).

God created humankind good and beautiful, conformed to God's goodness/will and wisdom. Through self-will/sin, humankind lost the beauty and goodness of its conformity to the goodness/will and wisdom of God. Jesus Christ, the perfect image and likeness of God, is the manifestation of God's glory, reflecting the beauty of God's goodness/will and wisdom ("who sees me, sees the Father"), and transfigures the defaced/deformed image and likeness of God in humankind.

John's basic themes provide a matrix for understanding the cosmic conflict in which the glory/beauty of God in and through Christ transfigures or "saves" humankind, liberating it from the ugliness and ultimate futility of self-will for the joy of communion in conformity with Beauty Itself/God. Each theme represents an aspect of the beauty/glory of God and the joy it evokes among all who are baptized into his life and mission of making all things beautiful. Each theme implies how we glorify God by enjoying God in the beauty/glory of his Son. Even now, within the eschatological tension of our historical pilgrimage and the cosmic conflict between the glorified Christ and the "prince of this world," we experience something of that joy and beauty.

The beauty of God's Word/meaning in Christ vs. meaninglessness
The beauty of God's Truth in Christ vs. unreality/mendacity
The beauty of God's Joy in Christ vs. desolation

The beauty of God's Love in Christ vs. hatred/unlove
The beauty of God's Life in Christ vs. death/lifelessness
The beauty of God's Sight in Christ vs. blindness
The beauty of God's Voice in Christ vs. deafness
The beauty of God's Way in Christ vs. aimlessness/wandering
The beauty of God's Glory in Christ vs. self-glorification
The beauty of God's Light in Christ vs. the darkness/alienation
The beauty of God's Knowledge in Christ vs. estrangement

The Gift and Call of God to Glory
(in the Glorified Christ)

The mysterious attractiveness of Jesus' person evokes the question of the first disciples: "Where do you live?" (1:38). The power of Jesus to draw us to himself (12:32) is conditioned by the prior drawing by the Father: "No one can come to me unless one is drawn by the Father who sent me" (6:44). And that prior drawing is a listening and a learning: "Everyone who has listened to the Father and learned from him, comes to me" (6:35). We cannot recognize the movement of the divine presence in the Son unless we are prepared for such recognition by the presence of the divine Father in ourselves.

The question of the first disciples does not concern Jesus' residence; rather, it concerns where and what his life is. Jesus lives "in the Father": "I am in the Father and the Father is in me" (14:10). (The same Greek verb, *menein*/to live, is used in both texts.)

"Come and see," the response of Jesus, invites the disciples to experience for themselves where Jesus lives: ". . . they went and saw where he lived, and stayed there with him the rest of the day" (1:39). Christian discipleship means both sharing Jesus' life in the Father and his mission of calling others to that life. The "come and see" of Jesus is what the Father speaks in God's incarnate Word. Jesus is the "come and see," the self-gift and call, the grace and invitation of the Father for all humankind. Jesus communicates the mysterious beauty/attractiveness/glory of the Father drawing all humankind to Godself.

The mysterious beauty of the Father drawing us to Godself in Jesus is shared by the disciples of Jesus. Philip, immediately after his welcoming the gift and call of Jesus, calls Nathanael to "come and see" Jesus (1:46). When Nathanael "sees" and proclaims that Jesus is the "Son of God" and the "king of Israel" (1:49), Jesus announces that he will see even greater things (1:50): "You will see heaven laid open and, above the Son of Man, the angels of God ascending and descending" (1:51). Alluding both to Jacob's ladder (Gen 28:12) and to Daniel's Son of Man (Dan 7:13-14), Jesus indicates that he is the mediator between God and humankind, the new Jacob's ladder through whom God descends to us and we ascend to God. In other words, Jesus is the way to meet/know God.

The same mysterious beauty/glory of the Father in Jesus transforms the Samaritan woman. Welcoming Jesus' revelation to her, "I am he" (4:26)—an allusion to the theophany Moses experienced (Exod 3:14)—the Samaritan woman tells the people, "Come and see" (4:30). In Jesus is now revealed the beauty/glory (John 1:14) whose reflection illuminated the face of Moses after his encounters with God (Exod 34:29-35). Whoever truly believes in Moses also believes in Jesus (John 5:45-47). His countenance, like that of Moses, reflects the beauty/glory of the Lord who transforms us into his own image (2 Cor 3:18). To see the glory of Jesus—"that is his as the only Son of the Father, full of grace and truth" (1:14)—entails both the revelation of the Father ("the only Son of the Father") and our salvation ("full of grace and truth").

Faith is the precondition for contemplating the beauty/glory of the Father's face and for enjoying the beauty of the Father's voice in Jesus: ". . . the Father who sent me bears witness to me himself. You have never heard his voice, you have never seen his face, and his word finds no home in you because you do not believe in the one he has sent" (5:37-38).

Mary Magdalene recognizes the risen Lord by the sound of his voice (20:16). She tells the disciples that she has seen the Lord (20:18). The sight of the risen Lord fills the disciples with peace and joy (20:20). Enjoying God's beauty/glory in the risen Lord is the distinguishing characteristic of all Christian life/experience.

Two Schemes of Gospel Thought

1. COSMIC CONFLICT IN JOHANNINE THOUGHT

Humanity was created "beautiful"—in the image and likeness of God. Through sin, humanity is *deformed* and becomes "ugly," losing this conformity with the will and wisdom of God. Jesus Christ, the perfect image of god, reflecting the splendor and beauty of the wisdom and goodness of God ("whoever sees me sees the Father"), *transforms* (transfigures) those deformed, making them, in himself and for himself, "beautiful" or perfectly *conformed* to God.

In the Johannine Writings, the cosmic conflict between Jesus Christ and the prince of this world, manifests the dialectic struggle between good and evil. At the heart of the eschatological struggle, in which God fights against and triumphs over the forces of evil that deform God's image and likeness in human beings. The Johannine themes provide a matrix and a key to understand how the glory and beauty of God in Jesus Christ transfigure the world, liberating it from its ugliness through the joy of communion or conformity with God, source of all beauty.

CONFLICT Cosmic struggle between Good and evil		Logos/Word	Each theme corresponds to the beauty of God in Christ. Each theme expresses an aspect of the joy of God that the beauty of Christ communicates.	Each theme corresponds to an aspect of the beauty of the life and mission of Christ, in which we are baptized to transfigure the universe with beauty.
absurdity			*Jesus Christ incarnates the meaning that God gives to life*	If we are in communion with Christ we are bearers of the meaning that God gives to life
lie	HUMANITY	Truth	*Jesus Christ is the eternal Truth*	If we are in Kingdom of Truth we help others to search and find the Truth
darkness		Light	*Jesus Christ is the Light that illumines and gives joy*	If we are in Christ our lives illumine and give joy to others
hatred	AS	Love	*Jesus Christ in his self-donation on the Cross is the triumph of invincible love over death and every evil*	If we are in Christ we communicate love
being lost	INDIVIDUAL	Way	*Jesus Christ is the only Way to eternal happiness*	If we are in communion with Christ Jesus our lives orient others towards eternal happiness
sadness	AND	Joy	*Jesus Christ is the Joy of God*	If we are in communion with Christ we are bearers of joy
blindness	AS	Vision	*Jesus Christ enjoys the vision of God*	If we are in Christ we communicate the joyful vision of the Father
deafness/ disobedience	SOCIETY	Listening/ Obedience	*Jesus Christ Listens and Obeys*	If we are in communion with Christ we listen and obey the Father
ignorance		Knowledge	*Jesus Christ Knows the Father*	If we are in Christ we communicate the knowledge of the Father
worldly vainglory/ self-glorification		Glory of God	*Jesus Christ is the Glory of the Father*	If we are in Christ we communicate the glory of God

2. The Holy Spirit of Reciprocal Love

The divine and human *pedagogy* for our *becoming the friends of God* entails the use of Scripture for both ascertaining Christian authenticity and promoting lifelong Christian conversion. The gift of the Holy Spirit of the Father and the Son is the foundation for the scriptural pedagogy of the Church; for we are not by nature participants in the divine nature, nor sharers in the inner life of the Trinity. It is only through the gift of God's love poured into our hearts that we have the "eye of love" (Christian faith) and the "look of love" (Christian contemplation) to "see" the beauty of the Church's scriptural iconography and to be transformed by its true meaning (1 Pet 1:4; Rom 5:5).

Each gospel underscores a complementary aspect of the Holy Spirit's transforming reciprocal love that is operative in Christian life and maturation.

MARK	MATTHEW	LUKE	JOHN
Evidences the Spirit of the Father's love for his beloved Son, which is the same Spirit of the Son's love for the Father in his total self-surrender on the cross. The Spirit of their reciprocal love enables us to share the Father's love for his beloved Son and the Son's love in total self-surrender to his Father. The gift of their Spirit enables all who welcome it to enjoy eternal life in the reciprocal love (Spirit) of the Father and the Son: eternal life/love	Evidences the Spirit of the Father's love for the community/ brothers and sisters/Church of his Son, which is the same Spirit as that of the Church's/ body of Christ's love for the Father. The Holy Spirit of the reciprocal love of Father and Son makes us both the sons and daughters of the Father and the brothers and sisters of the Son.	Evidences the Spirit of the Father's universal love for the entire world of his beloved Son, which is the same Spirit of the Son's all-encompassing love for the entire world of his Father. The Holy Spirit of their reciprocal love creates, sustains, unifies and transfigures all humankind as the Common Good of the universe.	Evidences the indwelling Spirit of the Triune God's reciprocal love which empowered the outgoing love that led us to love the Father and Son (Mark), the Body of Christ and the Temple of the Spirit/Church (Matt), and their universe/all creation (Luke).

The Gospels witness to the Holy spirit of reciprocal love in four complementary ways that ground Christian conversion as both event and lifelong process.

MARK witnesses to the reciprocal love (Holy Spirit) of the *Father and the Son*

MATTHEW witnesses to their reciprocal love both *for and within the Church*

LUKE–ACTS witnesses to their reciprocal love both *for and within the world*

JOHN witnesses to the *indwelling* reciprocal love of the Triune God as *the origin and ground and destiny of the outgoing love that Christians have* for the Triune God, the Church, and the world.

The *literary structure* of the Gospels implies that the Spirit of the Triune God's reciprocal love entails, among all who welcome it, a new life and its development. "Disciples" and "the Way of the Cross" are terms which indicate both the event and continual process of theocentric and Christocentric self-transcendence for becoming the "friends of God." We follow Christ in welcoming his Spirit of reciprocal love without limits.

Jesus reveals and communicates the Father's love for him, for his brothers and sisters (Church), and for the world/universe through the gift of their Holy Spirit of reciprocal love. The Father reveals God's self and communicates God's self in the beloved Son, in the community of the beloved Son, and in the universe of the beloved Son, through the gift of their Holy Spirit of reciprocal/theocentric/Christocentric/universal love as the trinitarian love that "trinifies" all things/creation. The "trinification" of all creation entails its transfiguration, divinization, a new creation.

5

The Universal Pilgrimage to the Mountain of God

Conversion Paradigm

The promise of a universal and eschatological fulfillment for humankind at the Mountain of God inspired the prophets of Israel and enabled the Christian community to grasp and to explain the meaning of that fulfillment in Jesus Christ and his life-giving death in Jerusalem (Mount Zion).

In the Old Testament Yahweh is "God of the mountains" (probable meaning of El-Shadday). In most religions mountains are considered to be the point where heaven and earth meet, where the gods dwell, or the place from which salvation comes. The Bible retains these beliefs but purifies them. Mountains are only one creature among many, and the "God of mountains" is also the God of valleys (1 Kgs 20:23). With Christ, God no longer wishes to be adored on this or that mountain, but in spirit and truth (John 4:20-24).

Mountains are associated with stability and power. Human beings pass, the mountains remain. Mountains become a symbol of God's faithfulness and reliability (Ps 36:7). The mountain offered Lot refuge in peril (Gen 19:17), and attracted the persecuted just who sought to flee there (Ps 11:1; Ezek 7:16; Matt 24:16). But the just must take care in raising their eyes to the mountains; for from God alone will they obtain their ultimate security (Ps 121:1-2; Jer 3:23).

In the Hebrew Bible (Old Testament) sacred mountains serve several functions in God's relationship with the people. The mountain, particularly Sinai and Zion, represented God's abode; it was the place on which God descended from heaven. The descent on the sacred mountain provided the means whereby God revealed God's personal name and identity to Moses, proclaimed God's will in terms of Torah and judgment or salvation, and commissioned leaders and kings to carry out his purposes.

New Testament writers continued this understanding of the sacred mountain but transformed its use and function to explain the identity and mission of Jesus. Not only did the specific announcement about his identity as God's son occur on a mountain, but the functions which Jesus performed on "the mountain" are the same as those attributed to God on the sacred mountains of the Hebrew Bible.[1]

The Universal Pilgrimage to the Mountain of God[2]

The idea of the Mountain of God as the goal of all nations is a very ancient one that Jewish prophets may have borrowed from the Jebusite Jerusalem cult. Isaiah envisions the eschatological pilgrimage of the Gentiles to the Mountain of God (Mt. Zion): "And it shall come to pass in the latter days, that the mountain of the Lord's house shall be established in the top of the mountains, and shall be exalted above the hills; and all the nations shall flow unto it; and many peoples shall go and say, Come, let us go up to the mountain of the Lord, to the house of the God of Jacob; and he will teach us his ways, and we will walk in his paths" (Isa 2:2-3, parallel in Micah 4:1).

---

[1] Some translations of the Greek New Testament lead the reader to miss the impact of "the mountain" because the Greek *to horos* is generalized by such renderings as "the hills," "the hill country," or "a hill." Yet, because of the actions which Jesus performed on *to horos,* the expression refers not to any hill or mountain but to the Mountain of God.

[2] John Navone, *Self-Giving and Sharing: The Trinity and Human Fulfillment* (Collegeville: The Liturgical Press, 1989) 12–18.

Five Aspects of the Universal Pilgrimage

There are five aspects of the universal pilgrimage to the Mountain of God that symbolically represent five moments or dimensions of religious conversion both as event and lifelong process in response to the grace and call of God.[3] We are not capable of *achieving* the total theocentric self-transcendence of religious conversion. Rather, we receive this type of ultimate theocentric self-transcendence as a gift. It is an otherworldly state of being in love with God that occurs within this world but goes beyond it, in which all values are placed in the light and the shadow of transcendent value, the Supreme Good that is God: in the shadow, for God is supreme and incomparable; in the light, for God is originating and all-encompassing goodness. Religious conversion is a state of an unconditioned being in love, since no finite object or person can be the object of such an unqualified love. Only of God can we truly say: "Without you I cannot live, love, or exist." God alone can be the object of a love that is without reserve or unconditioned in every respect. By defining religious conversion as "God's love flooding our hearts," Bernard Lonergan has made religious conversion the foundational reality for theology.[3] His conversion theology enlightens our understanding and appreciation of the biblical symbolism for the universal pilgrimage to the Mountain of God.

1. *The Epiphany of God.* The universal pilgrimage to the Mountain of God begins with God's self-revelation, epiphany, or theophany, corresponding to the moment when God becomes the center of our lives, when we become sharply aware of the difference between God and not-God, when the awesome *Mysterium tremendum* captures our attention.

The Hebrew Bible expresses diverse aspects of the first moment of epiphany/theophany. The nations are expectant: "The islands shall wait for me, and put their trust in my strength" (Isa 51:5).

---

[3] John Navone, *Self-Giving and Sharing,* chapter 3, "Conversion for Communion" explains Bernard Lonergan's views on conversion, 35–44. His conversion theology grounds my treatment and application of conversion to the pilgrimage symbolism.

Now they hold their breath in awe: "Let all humankind be silent before the Lord! For he is awaking and is coming from his holy dwelling" (Zech 2:13). The epiphany of God (theophany) occurs when the Mountain of the Temple will rise above all mountains and hills (Isa 2:2). The glory of God will be revealed to all the world (Isa 40:5). God's truth will appear as a light of the nations (Isa 51:4; 60:3); "The Lord bares his holy arm in the sight of all the nations" (Isa 52:10). A standard is displayed: "Make a way for the people. . . . Hoist the signal for the peoples" (Isa 62:10); "That day, the root of Jesse shall stand as a signal to the peoples of the world. It will be sought out by the nations and its home will be glorious" (Isa 11:10). Israel is the locus of the theophany for humankind.

2. *The Call of God.* The second moment of the universal pilgrimage to the Mountain of God is experienced as vocation; for theophany is always the experience of God's glory, splendor, attractiveness, allure. *Mysterium fascinans* captivates, enraptures, and grips us. Theophany/epiphany is not the experience of detached spectators; rather, it is the experience of those whom *Mysterium fascinans* attracts, draws, delights, allures, "fascinates" or "calls." There is no knowing God, in the biblical sense, apart from joy, marvel, awe, and peace. To experience the glory of God is to experience the call of God: the beauty of God's supreme goodness draws us to Godself.

The Hebrew Bible tells of the wonderful works of the Lord that draw or "call" this people to the Lord as to a loving Father (Hos 11) or caring Shepherd (Isa 40:11; 63:11-14; Ps 78:52). God's people marvel at the beauty of God's mercy and loving-kindness (Neh 9; Pss 78; 106; Ezek 20). God's holiness and glory shine forth to inspire and enrapture his people (Num 20:13).

God's word explains the meaning of "God's epiphany": "God, even God the Lord has spoken, and called the earth from the rising of the sun to its setting, from Zion, perfection of beauty he shines" (Ps 50:1). This divine command is addressed to the Gentiles: "Assemble, come, gather together, survivors of the nations. . . . Turn to me and be saved, all the ends of the earth, for I am God unrivaled" (Isa 45:20, 22). Israel, as God's instrument, echoes the call: "See, You will summon a nation you never knew, those unknown will come hurrying to you, for the sake of the Lord your God, of the Holy One of Israel who will glorify you" (Isa 55:5). "Proclaim his salvation day after day, tell of his glory among the nations, tell his marvels to every people. . . . Say among the nations, the Lord reigns!" (Ps 96:3, 10). The Gentiles, too, who have survived the divine judgment, proclaim the glory of God among the nations, and summon them to the pilgrimage to the Mountain of God (Isa 66:19-20). But God has yet another messenger, the Servant of the Lord, who not only restores the preserved of Israel, but whom God makes known as the light of the Gentiles (Isa 42:6; 49:6). The response to the call is:

3. *The Journey of the Gentiles.* The universal pilgrimage to the Mountain of God presupposes a common human nature under the sovereignty of a self-revealing, self-giving, and calling Lord, even though the revelation and call of God to all humankind has its locus in the people of Israel. The epiphany and the call of God set in motion a spiritual transformation or itinerary of growth and development for which "the journey of the Gentiles" is a metaphor. The God of Israel is the God of all humankind; that God's epiphany and call is for all humankind.

The Hebrew Bible describes the journey of the Gentiles in terms of a highway constructed straight through the Near East from Egypt and Assyria to Jerusalem (Isa 19:23). At the same time the summons is heard in the cities of the Gentiles: "Come, let us go up to the mountain of God" (Isa 2:3). "Come, let us go and entreat the favor of the Lord, and seek the Lord of hosts; I am going myself" (Zech 8:21). If there should happen to be a Jew of the Diaspora returning home, ten men out of all the languages of the nations will take hold of his garment and say: "We want to go with you, since we have heard that God is with you" (Zech 8:23). All the nations, led by their kings (Isa 60:11; Ps 47:10) stream toward Jerusalem, the throne of the Lord (Jer 3:17), in an unending procession "from sea to sea and from mountain to mountain" (Mic 7:12). Their shoulders are bent under the weight of the gifts that they bring (Isa 18:7; Hag 2:7; Ps 68:30, 32). The costly gifts the nations bring are described in the vivid imagery of Isaiah 60: the wealth of the seas

(v. 5), gold, silver, and incense (vv. 6, 9), borne upon camels and dromedaries (v. 6); then come animal victims for sacrifice upon God's altar (v. 7), the costly wood from Lebanon for building the temple (v. 13). They bear Israel's sons and daughters in their arms as a precious treasure (v. 6), "upon horses, and in chariots, and in litters, and upon mules and upon dromedaries, to my holy mountain Jerusalem, says the Lord (Isa 66:20). The gates are to be kept open day and night, "that men may bring you the wealth of the nations" (60:11). Those who are left out of all the nations come year by year to the feast of Tabernacles in Jerusalem to worship (Zech 14:16), even new moon after new moon they come, Sabbath after Sabbath (Isa 66:18). "They will come trembling from their lairs" (Mic 7:17), "bowing at your feet" (Isa 60:14). The goal of the universal pilgrimage is:

4. *Worship at the World-Sanctuary.* God's gracious self-revelation (epiphany/theophany) and call leads to the transforming dynamic of theocentric self-transcendence in all human beings undergoing the event and lifelong process of religious conversion. This process is symbolized by an ascent to the World-sanctuary, the House/Temple of God, on the Mountain of God, culminating in the worship of God above all: "My house will be a house of prayer for all the nations" (Isa 56:7). The ascent to the House of God symbolizes the universal imperative to love God above all as a prerequisite for human fulfillment and freedom under the sovereignty of God's love. The ascent implies the ongoing struggle to overcome the human propensity for self-idolatry in fidelity to the gift and call of God to friendship with God and all humankind (peace/*shalom*).

Isaiah affirms the universal call of God to worship in the world-sanctuary: "Even the Gentiles who have attached themselves to the Lord . . . will I bring to my holy mountain, and make them joyful in my house of prayer. Their holocausts and their sacrifices will be accepted on my altar, for my house will be called a house of prayer for all peoples" (Isa 56:7; Mark 11:17). All the ends of the earth shall turn to the Lord (Ps 22:28); they shall see the glory of God (Isa 66:18) in the courts of the world-sanctuary (Ps 96:8) and fall on their knees before him (Isa 45:23). Moreover, God will cleanse their lips "that they may call upon the name of the Lord" (Zeph

3:9). With cleansed lips they will confess: "Our fathers inherited nothing but Delusion, Nothings void of power, (Jer 16:19), and add their tribute of praise: "You alone are great, you perform marvels, you God, you alone" (Ps 86:10); "From the Lord alone comes victory and strength" (Isa 45:24). A description of this act of adoration is given when the Sabaean prisoners of war will be brought in chains by the Persians to Jerusalem, praying as they pass: "With you alone is God, and he has no rival; there is no other god" (Isa 45:14). The worship addressed to God is accompanied by homage to the messianic king (Ps 72:9-11), and to the People of God (Isa 49:23), bearers of blessing for the world (Isa 19:24). The divine response to the adoration of the Gentiles is expressed in the amazing universal blessing: "Blessed by Egypt, my people, Assyria, the work of my hands, and Israel, my inheritance" (Isa 19:25).

5. *The Messianic Banquet on the Mountain of God.* The culmination of the universal pilgrimage to the Mountain of God is the communion, community, and communication of all humankind in joy and friendship under the lordship of God's love. To the extent that individuals, societies, and nations are their own "little gods," universal peace, love, and reconciliation are impossible. The Great Commandment implies that only by letting God be God, by loving God above all, are we free to love others as ourselves. We are, otherwise, condemned to a state of endless civil war in which each little god clashes with other little gods to be the center and ultimate purpose of the human story. As a human community, to paraphrase St. Augustine, we cannot rest (or have the joy of peace) until we rest in God. Divine and human friendship in the kingdom of God is the culmination and perfection of religious conversion.

The eschatological banquet community is the gift of God, established through the agency of God's Messiah. The prophets of Israel proclaimed that the Messiah would inaugurate eschatological peace and happiness among the poor and the afflicted who would form his banquet community (Isa 25:6; 34:6; 55:1; Zeph 1:7). The banquet metaphor expresses messianic salvation for all humankind in terms of God's gracious hospitality and all-encompassing love.

The eschatological banquet of all nations on the Mountain of God expresses the truth that all humankind belongs to the People of God under the peaceful reign of the Messiah (Zech 9:10) and the dominion of the Son of Man (Dan 7:14). In all the Jewish Bible's references to the eschatological pilgrimage of the Gentiles, the goal is the holy Mountain of God, Zion, where God reveals Godself. The Gentiles will be summoned to the holy Mountain for the divine epiphany. The redemption celebrated at the banquet is that of Israel, revealed to the Gentiles, who are now included in God's redeemed community.

The communion of the banquet community as mediating the vision of God is an ancient element of biblical symbolism that runs through the Bible from beginning (Gen 3:22) to end (Rev 22:17). It is of fundamental importance for grasping the meaning of all statements in apocalyptic literature and in the New Testament about the universal messianic eschatological banquet.

> On this mountain,
> The Lord of hosts will prepare for all peoples
> a banquet of rich food, a banquet of fine wines,
> of food rich and juicy, of fine strained wines.
> On this mountain he will remove,
> the mourning veil covering all peoples,
> and the shroud enwrapping all nations,
> he will destroy Death for ever.
> The Lord of hosts will wipe away
> the tears of every cheek;
> he will take away his people's shame
> everywhere on earth,
> for the Lord has said so.
> That day, it will be said: See, this is our God
> in whom we hoped.
> We exult and we rejoice
> that he has saved us;
> for the hand of the Lord
> rests on this mountain (Isa 25:6-10).

New Testament Fulfillment of Pilgrimage Prophecy

The five basic aspects of the Jewish Bible's universal pilgrimage prophecy symbolize the religious conversion of the Gentiles to the God of Israel. The same five aspects have their counterpart in the New Testament's symbolic interpretation of Christian conversion to the God of Israel as revealed in Jesus Christ.

1. *Epiphany/Christophany/Theophany.* The gospel narratives of the passion and death of Jesus resume the theme of God's self-revelation on the Mountain of God, Zion. The Roman centurion is the first person to make the full Christian confession of faith: Jesus is the Son of God (15:39). That the first Christian confession of faith should come from a Gentile symbolizes the universal scope and efficacy of the Messiah or Servant of God who gives his life for all. The centurion is the spokesman for the Christian faith and for the Gentiles who are called by God to join the Jews as the People of God. The universal revelation and call of God occurs in the death of Jesus on the Mountain of God, Zion. The tearing of the temple veil in two, from top to bottom (Mark 15:38), represents the ultimate theophany, the divine self-disclosure as christophany. The very God whose "face" or presence was veiled within the holy of holies (Exod 33:11, 14) rips away the veil to show his "face" and to manifest his presence in Jesus Christ.

2. *The Call of God in Christ.* In John's Gospel, Jesus is the incarnate Word of God expressing the universal call of God to "come and see" (1:38). He expresses the call of God to the communion, community, and communication of friendship: "I have called you friends" (15:15).

John's description of Jesus as the Good Shepherd also implies the call of God in Jesus Christ. The Greek adjective that John uses to qualify shepherd is *kalos,* which means "beautiful," "morally good," "attractive," or "lovely." Jesus is The "Beautiful" Shepherd who lays down his life for his sheep (10:11). The beauty of his self-giving love will "draw all persons to himself" (12:32). And this beauty of his goodness is supremely seen in the act by which he would so draw them, wherein he lays down his life for his sheep. The beauty of God's love in The "Beautiful" Shepherd saves the world.

Matthew's saying about the lamp which is not to be placed under a bushel (5:14) implies that "the city set on a hill" is the city of God on the Mountain of God whose glory cannot remain hidden. Matthew (also Mark 4:21; Luke 8:16; 11:33) implies that Jesus is the eschatological light shining forth as the revelation of God to summon all humankind to the Mountain of God.

3. *Jesus Is the Way* (John 14:4). Jesus is the Way to the communion with God that is the goal of the universal pilgrimage to the Mountain of God. His Way of the Cross is God's way of self-giving love that constitutes life in the kingdom.

Luke's Gospel depicts the public ministry of Jesus as the way (13:33) of divine necessity for the accomplishment of God's universal salvation: "It is necessary for me to be on my way today and tomorrow and the day following, for it is impossible that a prophet should die outside Jerusalem." The Spirit leads the way for the accomplishment of the divine purpose (4:1, 14). The way of the Lord is identical with the way of Jesus (3:4; 7:27). Through the gift of his Spirit the risen Christ abides with his people and guides them along the way of the Lord for the salvation of all humankind (Acts 4:30; 5:12; 6:8; 14:3; 15:12).

4. *Jesus Is the Temple/Universal Sanctuary of God.* Mark affirms through the symbolism of the torn veil of the Temple at the death of Jesus (15:38) that God has created a direct access to Godself for all humankind in Jesus, the Son, the Beloved (1:11; 9:7). Jesus replaces the Temple as the center or locus of divine holiness. This is the point of the accusation at his trial: "We heard him say 'I will destroy this temple made by human hands and in three days build another, not made by human hands'"(14:58). Jesus is the world-sanctuary in and through whom God is to be recognized and worshiped by all humankind. The Temple veil no longer hides God's glory. Through the death of Jesus all humankind can see the glory of God in the crucified, who has established a new people in fulfillment of the prophecy: "My house shall be called a house of prayer for all the nations" (11:17).

Both Ezekiel (34:23-24) and Micah (5:2-4) refer to a future shepherd who will feed the sheep of God. The Gospels tell of the scattered Gentile flock of God's people (Matt 25:32; John 10:16; 11:51-52). The eschatological gathering of the nations will take place at the new Temple of God on Mount Zion, where God is truly known, loved, and worshiped.

5. *Jesus' Eschatological Messianic Banquet.* The message of Jesus promising salvation to the Gentiles summarizes the Hebrew Bible's utterances about the eschatological pilgrimage of the Gentiles to the Mountain of God at the time of the Last Judgment: "I say to you, they shall come in countless numbers from the east and from the west, and will sit down with Abraham, Isaac, and Jacob in the kingdom of heaven while the sons of the kingdom will be cast into outer darkness" (Matt 8:11-12 = Luke 13:28-29). Jesus recalls two passages from Isaiah: "Lo, these shall come from far: and, lo, these from the north and from the west" (49:12); and the description of the banquet that the Lord has prepared for all humankind on his holy mountain (25:6-10). The messianic banquet expresses the divine redemption in which the Gentiles will feast with the patriarchs, who represent the People of God. The Gentiles are incorporated into the People of God at the consummation of all things. The note of universal salvation is implied in all the parables and sayings of Jesus that speak of the eschatological banquet. Jesus speaks of this banquet under such symbols as the wedding feast, as the high festival that awaits the faithful and wise servant (Matt 25:21, 23), as the final Passover (Luke 22:16), as the satisfying of all hunger (Matt 5:6 = Luke 6:21). This banquet is the feast upon Mount Zion described in Isaiah, God's universal feast toward which the nations flow, where the veil that shrouds them, and the covering that blinds their eyes, shall be rent asunder.

There are remarkable correspondences between Mark's account of the passion and death of Jesus and the messianic banquet prophecy of Isaiah 25:6-10: the mountain/Zion; the divine initiative; the Messiah through whom God achieves his ends; the eschatological banquet/Last Supper; the universal scope of the event "for all"; the removal of the veil/tearing of the Temple veil; the triumph over death; the removal of the people's shame; the divine judgment, on "that day" of God's once-and-for-all intervention for our liberation and salvation; the revelation of God and his salvation; joy in the fulfillment of human hopes.

Only those who have the eye of faith for theophany/christophany and the ears that hear the call of God participate in the universal pilgrimage to the Mountain of God. Conversion in the ascent to the Mountain of God is always precarious; for eyes may fail to see and ears may fail to hear the God who invites all humankind to the eternal joy and happiness of the banquet that God has prepared for those who love God.

Excursus: Jesus the Way

The metaphor of Jesus as the Way implies that he is both the way of God to humankind and the way of humankind to God. From the standpoint of the Christian community's spiritual journey, Jesus is the Alpha and the Omega of God's saving way. He is the preexistent *logos*/Word, the incarnate Word, the risen Christ. He begins from Galilee, follows the Way of the Lord through Palestine, and finishes his work in Jerusalem. The Christian follows Jesus' "way to life" (Acts 2:28), obedient to the injunction to take up the Cross daily and follow him (Luke 9:23).

There is a threefold temporal dimension to Jesus' journey: "It is necessary for me to be on my way today and tomorrow and the day following, for it is impossible that a prophet should die outside Jerusalem" (Luke 13:33). Jesus is sent by the Father and returns to the Father as the first of many brothers. He is the New Adam, recalling another journey pattern: Paradise Lost (Garden), the Desert Wilderness, and Paradise Regained. Israel had experienced its homecoming (the Return) after its Babylonian Exile (587–37 B.C.E.), Egyptian tyranny, a desert wandering, and entrance into a Promised Land had marked its first homecoming. The Parable of the Prodigal Son is another travel story with three parts: a rupture of relations with a departure from the Father, an "exile" of riotous living in a foreign land, a remembering and returning to the Father. In this parable, the return includes the notion of the land where the Father dwells (fatherland). Such homecoming implies mutual recognition and acceptance, and that state where we are most ourselves, where we have life most fully. The Latin word for homeland or native country is fatherland *(patria),* the place where our father(s) dwells, our origins. If our seeing Jesus is our seeing the Father (John 14:9), it is our faith that sees the Way home.

Jesus Christ is the origin and ground and goal of Christian development. In Augustine's words, "he is our native country." He is the criterion of our development, for "he made himself also the way to that country" (*On Christian Doctrine,* trans. D. W. Robertson, Jr., Indianapolis, 1958, p. 64). The Christian grows both in Christ and to Christ. As Augustine remarks in *Christian Doctrine* (p. 13), the Christian life is "a journey or voyage home." Luther shares the same view: "For it is not sufficient to have done something, and now to rest . . . this present life is a kind of movement and passage, a transition . . . a pilgrimage from this world into the world to come, which is eternal rest" (quoted by Gerhard Ebeling, *Luther: An Introduction to His Thoughts,* trans. R. A. Wilson, Philadelphia, 1970, 161–62).

In calling himself "the way, the truth, and the life," the Johannine Christ was describing his own saving work in relation to humankind. He is the way to be followed; he is the revealer of truth; he is the source of abundant life.

First, truth. The revelation of truth belongs to the prophet and teacher that is Christ. The truth of Christ removes a veil, letting reality be seen as it is in God's eyes. Only so can we get our bearings and live authentically. As "the light of the world," (John 1:9; 8:12; 12:46), Christ opposed lies, deceit, and illusion, which are the consequence of sin (John 1:5; 3:19; 8:44).

Second, life. The giving of life belongs to the priestly office of Christ. Life is always more than purely biological life; life includes us and our questions about life, about authentic, fulfilled, true life. Life longs for the light of life, and that light is an essential factor in life itself. But since life is constantly threatened by decay and death, the question of true life includes the question of abiding, eternal life. God's life appeared in Jesus Christ (John 1:4; 5:26; 11:25; 10:10). By giving his life, his self-sacrifice, Jesus is both sacrificial victim and sacrificing priest. Only then is flesh given for the life of the world (John 6:51); and "he who eats my flesh and drinks my blood has eternal life, and I will raise him up at the last day" (John 6:54).

Third, the way. The way of truth and life is a royal road; and direction belongs to the king, guidance to the shepherd. In the Jewish Bible, the Lord is Israel's king (Exod 15:18; Pss 95–99; 145; 146) and shepherd (Gen 49:24; Ps 23:1). In the Fourth Gospel, Jesus is "the good shepherd," who "lays down his life for his sheep" (John 10:11-18); he is the "king of the Jews," who "bears witness to the truth" (John 18:33-37). He goes ahead to prepare a place for his followers, that where he is, there they may be also (John 14:2-3). Lifted up, he is drawing all people to himself (John 12:32).

Excursus, Part II:
From Paradise Lost to Paradise Regained:
The Garden and the Wilderness Metaphors

The garden and the wilderness are two metaphors the Bible employs for describing the human condition. In the first creation Adam is provided the Garden of Eden or paradise as a perfect abode or workplace (Gen 2). The new Jerusalem (Rev 21) is described as the ideal joining of garden and city. The city of God descended from heaven has a river of life issuing from beneath God's throne, much as a fountain arises in the midst of Eden's garden. The river is lined with trees whose fruit is for nourishment and whose leaves are for the healing of all the nations.

The garden of God in Eden represents the harmony, peace, abundance, beauty, security, and delight that characterizes the communion, community, and communication of God and humankind. The garden of God represents how God intended human life to be lived. The Garden of Eden (Gen 2:8) represents a way of life and a state of soul under the sovereignty of the gracious God who has planted it. It is an image of divine provision and human collaboration; for the garden of God requires cultivation. It does not, therefore, represent the paradisiacal condition of humankind as one of indolence and inertia. God has put Adam in the Garden of Eden to till it and keep it (Gen 2:15). God has prepared the garden for human industry, work, and striving. The presence of the Tree of Life suggests that the garden of God represents the ideal condition for abundant human life and development. Humankind is enjoined to collaborate in obedience to God's unfolding purpose.

God visits the garden that God has planted, "walking in the garden in the cool of the day" (Gen 3:8). The garden of God represents the harmony and friendship of God and humankind. The expulsion of Adam and Eve from Eden results from the breakdown of their communion of friendship with God.

The two gardens of Jesus' life are associated with the meaning of his death and resurrection for the restoration of divine and human friendship in God's new creation. The garden of Gethsemane is the place of suffering and betrayal, or arrest and violence. It represents the cost of God's self-giving love in the radical decision of Jesus Christ that reverses the course of human history.

The garden of the resurrection is the place of the tomb near the site of the crucifixion (John 19:41). Mary Magdalene, at one level of meaning, "mistakes" the risen Jesus for the gardener (John 20:15). In the light of Christian faith, Mary Magdalene is not mistaken; for Christ is the New Adam of the new creation, who cultivates the garden of God as God's "gardener." Through the death and resurrection of Jesus Christ, God has restored humankind to the communion of friendship that was divine and human life in the first creation. The first garden accommodated the first Adam; the Easter garden accommodates the second Adam. As Paul exclaims, "If, because of the one man's trespass, death reigned through that one, much more surely will those who receive the abundance of grace . . . reign in life through the one man, Jesus Christ" (Rom 5:17 RSV). The resurrection offers a new horizon for humankind, with a world defined not by death but by life, with the prospect of growth into the fullness of the stature of Christ.

The Jesus of Luke's Gospel answers the prayer of the Christian community of faith as represented by the Good Thief with the promise that "today, you shall be with me in Paradise" (23:43). The communion of friendship with God is the ultimate meaning of paradise of life in the garden of God, which the crucified and risen Christ makes available to all humankind.

The Wilderness Metaphor

Among most early cultures paradise represented the greatest human good; the wilderness, its antipode, represented the greatest evil. In the first condition the environment ministered to every human desire ("Eden" is the Hebrew word for "delight"). Human happiness, security, and development all seemed dependent on rising out of the dangerous wilderness condition (see Deut 8:15).

The wilderness in Jewish Scriptures is a cursed land which becomes the condition of sinful humankind in its alienation from god. As a punishment for their disobedience Adam and Eve are driven from Eden into the wilderness, a cursed land full of thorns and thistles. The identification of the wilderness with God's curse led to the belief that it was a kind of hell populated by malign spirits, by all the menacing forces which upset, oppress, and play havoc with the human spirit (see Lev 16:22; Isa 13:21; 34:14). The wilderness was often a place of immorality, anarchy, chaos, death, decay, and desolation (see Jer 3:2).

The wilderness is associated with rebellion against God (Num 27:14; Ezek 20:13-21). It is a punishment for faithlessness (Num 14:32-33; Deut 9:28). The wilderness wandering becomes one of the central themes of Jewish history (Job 12:24; Ps 106:26; Ezek 20). The wilderness (wasteland, desert) is a central image for alienation from God, from neighbor, and from self. Persons are "bewildered" in an alien environment where the civilization that normally orders and controls human life is absent. Such an environment produces a state of mind in which persons feel lost, stripped of guidance, perplexed, and at the mercy of alien, mysterious, and malign forces. Wilderness is the environment of the nonhuman and antihuman where human persons are aliens. It is a region where persons are likely to get into a disordered, confused, or "wild" condition.

Wilderness, for Christians, has long been a powerful symbol applied either to the moral chaos of the unregenerate or to the godly person's conception of life on earth as a pilgrim in an alien land struggling against temptations endangering one's spiritual life. Jesus affirms that he is the Way (John 14:4-6), with the implication that he liberates us from the wilderness condition for the fullness of life of "today . . . in paradise" (Luke 23:43).

The garden and wilderness are biblical metaphors for the pulls and counterpulls that we experience in our quest for happiness. The crucified and risen Christ, who has shared the tensional structure of our condition in all but sin, promises to be with us until the end of time (Matt 28:20) to free us from the wilderness/wasteland condition of paradise lost for eternal happiness in the paradise that he has regained for us.

The Universal Pilgrimage to the Mountain of God as a Paradigm of the Universal Call to Conversion

The symbolism of the Mountain of God is found throughout sacred Scripture: Abraham's sacrifice on Mount Moria (Gen 22:2) where Solomon eventually builds the temple (2 Chr 3:1); Moses receives the Law on Mount Sinai; Mount Zion (Ps 68:16); Mount Carmel (Elijah–1 Kgs 18; 2 Kgs 4:25); Mount Tabor; the Mount of Beatitudes; the Mount of Olives, and Calvary.

At the heart of the Mountain of God symbolism is the conviction that the God who is love is calling all humankind to eternal happiness under the sovereignty of God's love. In the Old Testament, the mountain of God is predominately Mount Zion. The prophet Isaiah describes the eschatological pilgrimage to the Mountain of God:

> And it shall come to pass in the last days, that the mountain of the Lord's house shall be established in the top to the mountains, and shall be exalted above the hills; and all nations shall flow into it. And many people shall go, and say, Come, let us go up to the mountain of the Lord, to the house of the God of Jacob (Isa 2:2-3).

Old Testament eschatological prophecy	*New Testament fulfillment*
5 stages of the pilgrimage	5 stages of Christian pilgrimage
1. The universal pilgrimage to the Mountain of God begins with a theophany/epiphany (God's self-revelation (cf. Isa 2:1-2).	1. The christophany at the crucifixion evokes the centurion's confession of faith initiating the Christian pilgrimage.
2. The call of God—*Mysterium fascinans*—draws/attracts/inspires the pilgrimage. The universal vocation is evoked by the divine beauty/glory (Ps 50:1-6).	2. Jesus is the grace and call of God for universal friendship: "Come and see" (John 1:38); "I have called you friends" (John 15:15).
3. The pilgrimage of humankind is set in motion by the self-giving (theophany) and attractiveness (beauty) of God (Mic 7:12).	3. Jesus is the Way (John 14:6) to God. His Way of the Cross is God's way of self-giving love that constitutes life in the kingdom under the sovereignty of God's all-encompassing love.

4. The ascent to the universal sanctuary/temple of God on the Mountain of God culminates in worship of God above all: "My house will be a house of prayer for the nations" (Isa 56:7).	4. Jesus is the Universal Sanctuary/Temple of God in whom God is truly known, loved, and worshiped.
5. The Messiah establishes the eschatological banquet community on the mountain of God for all humankind under the sovereignty of God's love (Isa 25:6-10): the peace and joy of God for all.	5. Jesus is the Messiah whose eschatological banquet community is the ultimate fulfillment and happiness of all humankind under the sovereignty of God's love.

The way of the disciple

1. Epiphany: When we become aware of God's presence in our lives.

2. The Call: The attractiveness of God's presence draws/interests/holds us.

3. The Spiritual Journey or pilgrimage is set in motion in response to both the theophany/God's self-revelation and its beauty *(Mysterium fascinans)*.

4. The Ascent to the Sanctuary/Temple on the Mountain of God: Theocentric/Christocentric self-transcendence in loving God above all fulfills the first part of the Great Commandment.

5. Eschatological Banquet Community on the Mountain of God: Only when we love God above all are we free to enjoy communion with all others in fulfillment of the second part of the Great Commandment.